The Moment of Truth

Women's Funniest Romantic Catastrophes

Edited By Kristin Beck

Seal Press

THE MOMENT OF TRUTH:
Women's Funniest Romantic Catastrophes

Compilation copyright © 2002 by Kristin Beck

Published by Seal Press
An Imprint of Avalon Publishing Group Incorporated
161 William St., 16th Floor
New York, NY 10038

Library of Congress Cataloging-in-Publication Data
is available for this title.

ISBN 1-58005-069-7

9 8 7 6 5 4 3 2

Interior design by Susan Canavan

Printed in the United States of America
Distributed by Publishers Group West

Contents

Acknowledgments

My sincere gratitude goes, first and foremost, to the talented writers included in this collection. Every one of these women was a pleasure to work with. I'd like to thank the remarkable women at Seal Press: Senior Editor Leslie Miller, girl-genius and friend, went far beyond the call of duty with this project— I share it with her . . . and also Christina Henry, Rosemary Caperton, Anne Mathews, Faith Conlon, Ingrid Emerick, and Lynn Siniscalchi. Thanks also to Jennie Goode for her fine copyediting. To my family—Beck and Liotta versions both—I am grateful once again for the solid baseline support and encouragement. Thanks to sweet friends near and far, especially Carole Honeychurch, whose warmth and jokes are more rejuvenating than a full night's sleep. My deepest appreciation and love goes to Andy Liotta, who has sheltered me from many of the horrors detailed in this book. Cormac, you are my heart. Maude, don't plan on dating until you're thirty.

Foreword

There was the time I rolled over to his side of the bed and onto the floor because he wasn't in his accustomed place to act as a stopper. It was my moment of truth. I blamed him for my shoulder injury because this was just the last and most literal of one too many times I counted on him and he wasn't there for me.

Or the recent day the bride and groom's nearest and dearest stood shivering in the gloom of a San Francisco Bay–area summer afternoon, gathered together for a romantic outdoor wedding in a redwood grove. My on-again, off-again beau stood behind me, wrapping his arms around my shoulders and pressing into my back in a most uncharacteristically salacious manner. I grinned up at him with surprised delight. He looked back, unsmiling, and explained, "I'm just cold." And of course, I accepted that, finally and irrefutably, as truth.

And then there was . . . ah, but this is not about my experiences with pivotal relationship moments, but about yours . . . and hers . . . about all of ours, really. Pick a name out of anyone's romantic history. There isn't one of us who can't come up with some terrible and/or terrific tale attached to that object of affection, no matter how fleeting the fling. Even if we have to go all the way back to second grade, each one of us has a story or several of that one moment that allowed us an appalled glance at what Kristin Beck, the editor of this rowdy collection, calls "the nasty but hilarious underbelly of coupledom." If we didn't laugh, we'd cry.

I don't think there is a one of us who hasn't done that too, of course. Women's lot, and all that. But it is as human a need to find comfort and company in laughter as in our tears. I think the success of my long-running sex and relationship column, "Ask Isadora," has much to do with the relieved sighs of readers I call the "sexual unicorns," those who think their plight is uniquely their own. Seeing the agonized letters of others, they can sigh: *Whew, I am not the only one on Earth who (a) fell for a geek, (b) took so long to figure it out or (c) got ignominiously dumped.* Even more of a relief is realizing that however dreadful *it* was, any of the awful *it*s, someone else had it worse: *At least I didn't (a) fall in love with a two-timing loser, (b) lose my dessert as well as my dignity or (c) get dumped quite so flamingly in public* . . . This kind of crisis sharing, this communal "let's laugh and cry together and feel better," is also the nitty-gritty of this book.

Ah, the stories we could tell! And in this lovely collection, some of us do. No sexual unicorn, you!

—Isadora Alman

San Francisco, California

Dead Girl

Gina Ranalli

S ometimes, I still dream about a Dead girl.

I knew she was one of those Dead fans the moment I saw her stroll into the thrift store where I worked. She showed all the signs. Tie-dyed T-shirt with prancing skeletons. Old denim cut-offs with blotches of white from some long-ago bleach accident. Beat-up leather sandals.

Spying from behind a rack of clothes that smelled of cigars and musty old men, I watched her approach the front counter and fill out an application. She was tiny, about five feet tall and maybe, *maybe,* a hundred pounds. Raging red hair, thick and

1

glossy, hung past her shoulders and curled under at the ends. Unusually pale skin and eyes like big blue Valiums.

She was gorgeous.

But I had to get back to work and I promptly forgot all about her until the following morning, when she was back. Of course she'd been hired. Pretty much anyone who applied got hired, short of one or two violent criminals, though the boss was not averse to hiring *nonviolent* criminals. We were surrounded by more than a couple of those guys.

The boss introduced Dayna to the rest of us in the back room while we picked through bags upon bags of people's ancient unloved rags. We wore latex gloves to sort the salvageable from unsalvageable; some of it was *that* nasty. People would actually donate their crusty old underwear, complete with skid marks, and act as if we should be grateful to have it. We weren't.

Dayna nervously eyed everyone at the sorting tables. I don't know whether we, the workers as a group, worried her, or if she was just put off by the sight of all those discarded garments, most of which had belonged to people who were now decomposing in coffins.

I caught her eye and offered her a friendly smile. She still looked pretty scared but managed to smile back just before she was told to hang with Maria, a stout middle-aged Latina who would teach her the fine art of trash evaluation.

I went about my business, wondering vaguely if the new girl was gay but already pretty certain she wasn't. There were no vibes. I figured she was just what she appeared to be: a Deadhead hippie chick, young and pretty and straight.

Ah, well. What're you gonna do? Luck hadn't been on my side that summer, and there was no reason to think it would change anytime soon. Which was just as well. I wasn't looking for a relationship anyway. I'd just come out of one of those, a long one that had ended badly and left me emotionally scarred and exhausted. The most I was interested in was a close friendship with a dash of lovin' thrown in to keep things entertaining. Wishful thinking, I know.

My path didn't cross with Dayna's again until the next day, when I found her in the break room at lunchtime, sitting alone, nibbling a tuna sandwich and reading a Tom Robbins novel. It was the novel that caught my attention: *Even Cowgirls Get the Blues*. One of my favorites.

I sat down across from her with my gallon of sugary iced coffee and mentioned I loved Robbins but most especially

Cowgirls. She was shy at first, but eventually I got her to warm up with talk of the adventures of Sissy and Jellybean. She was convinced those characters would have lived happily ever after had it not been for Jellybean's death, a contention I held myself. It was her openness to this theory that made me wonder if maybe she *was* gay, after all.

After we'd said everything we could about the book, we sat in silence for a while, as Dayna finished her sandwich and I chugged down as much caffeine as I possibly could in the half-hour that remained of our break.

It wasn't until we headed back to the sorting room that Dayna asked me if I liked the Grateful Dead.

I shrugged. "I like some of their stuff."

"Which ones?" she asked, her blue eyes flashing intensely. My answer seemed important to her.

"I don't know," I laughed. "I guess I don't know too much of their music."

"Oh," she said, sounding disappointed.

"I really like 'Dark Star,'" I added quickly, hoping for a smile. I'd already decided I *loved* this girl's smile. "And 'High Time.' That's a good tune."

Bingo. The smile, slow and blooming, was back. I frantically racked my brain for other Dead songs, but I had a mental freeze and then she was walking away, back toward the table where Maria waited.

" 'Truckin'!" I called after her like an idiot. "Of course, I love 'Truckin'!"

The entire motley crew of the back room turned and gave me odd looks, and a couple of the guys loudly sang a few lines from that, the most famous of Dead songs. I waved them off and went back to work with tiny quivers of excitement simmering in my belly.

Over the next several weeks, Dayna and I became work friends, spending as much time together as possible while we raked through mounds and mounds of clothing, knickknacks, books, records and even furniture and appliances. We discovered all the things we had in common: We were close to the same age, and we'd both grown up in the city where we now worked, having returned after many years away. We both loved to read and began trading books back and forth, spending our lunch hours discussing and debating everything from *A Tale of Two Cities* to *Zen and the Art of Motorcycle Maintenance*. And, much to my surprise and delight, we were both indeed single lesbians.

It wasn't until Dayna actually invited me to her apartment that we discovered all the things we *didn't* have in common, the most obvious being the Grateful Dead.

I'd been amused when I first saw her car, a poor, physically abused Ford Escort, completely covered in Dead bumper stickers. Dayna had traveled the country in that rasping old heap, following her favorite band from sea to shining sea, and it showed. It was actually difficult to determine the color of the car beneath the psychedelic collage that wallpapered it. I'd learned that her car was famous in and around our small suburban city, but this knowledge had not prepared me for her house.

Let's just say that when I walked through her front door, I noticed she had a theme going. Everywhere I looked were dancing bears, skeletons and likenesses of Jerry Garcia. Every wall was decorated with posters and tapestries; she had framed various other collectibles as well, including an autographed bra, Grateful Dead Comix and countless ticket stubs. A vanity license plate reading GR8FL GRL hung over shelves where collector's plates and mugs were displayed. There was no surface not scattered with candles, incense holders and clocks, light switch covers and glued puzzles.

I stood in the center of this monsoon of swirling color, agape from sensory overload. Dayna stood beside me, grinning with pride. I looked down at her, petite and beautiful girl that she was, and said, "Jesus, you're fucking *insane.*"

She laughed. "Wait till you see the rest of the apartment."

"I'm not sure I want to." And I wasn't, but of course I had to be polite. I really liked her.

So I feigned fascination as she took me on the official tour of the Church of Jerry. Naturally, the last stop on the tour was her bedroom, where I discovered that she did indeed enjoy something other than the Dead.

After the dirty deed was done, we dozed for a while and when I woke, the first thing I saw was the red-white-and-blue Steal Your Face skull tattooed on Dayna's shoulder blade. She sat on the edge of the bed, her back to me, doing something I couldn't see. Completely engrossed in her task, she jumped when I touched her. When she turned, I saw that she was holding one of my Chuck Taylor All Star basketball sneakers in one hand and a Sharpie permanent marker in the other.

Puzzled, I asked what she was doing, though it was pretty obvious.

She smiled mischievously and held out the sneaker for my

inspection. I took it and blinked my groggy eyes at the new graffiti covering the white canvas.

"Mmm," I said and read aloud, " 'Is it live or is it dead?' Oh, and you drew a little skeleton in a top hat. Cute." The other sneaker was decorated with tiny roses and asked the question, "Are you kind?"

I studied my newly defaced Chucks with a twinge of annoyance, but then Dayna climbed on top of me, all downy legs and soapy scent, all soft and delicious, and I completely forgot about being irritated with her. Tranquilized by her Valium eyes, I almost managed to forget about Jerry Garcia gazing down at us from his spot on the ceiling, his face mildly amused and full of timeless wisdom. I couldn't help thinking he knew something I didn't and it was this secret knowledge that kept him smirking and giddy with glee. Or maybe he just had a head full of acid and was watching all the pretty colors streak by. I figured with old Jerry, it could probably go either way.

It didn't take long for me to grow tired of being surrounded by Dead memorabilia and persuade Dayna to hang out at my place instead. She was fairly easy to convince once I mentioned that I hated leaving my dog alone. Dayna adored her two cats, Cosmic Charlie and Tennessee Jed, so she understood completely when I claimed I missed Jude, my shepherd-collie, and felt guilty about leaving her alone. And I *did* feel guilty, but mostly I just wanted to look at my Dead-free walls and listen to my Dead-free stereo and spend some time in my own Dead-free world.

Initially Dayna was a great sport about being away from all her cherished mementos, but after a few nights in my apartment I could sense the withdrawal getting to her. She suddenly became very generous in the gift-giving department. I was amazed one night to actually hear myself saying, "Wow! These Grateful Dead salt and pepper shakers will look great on the counter beside my spider plant!"

And because I'd so convincingly simulated delight at receiving half a dozen little Dead trinkets, Dayna decided to give me something "extra-special" when our two-month anniversary rolled around.

After an excellent dinner and too many margaritas in our favorite Mexican restaurant, we went back to her apartment, and Dayna, adorably buzzed and excited, presented me with a Grateful Dead skateboard.

My eyes must have widened considerably because her enthusiasm abruptly melted into a crestfallen frown. "You don't like it?"

"Uh . . . yeah! Yes, I love it. It's beautiful." And it really did have beautiful paintings on both sides; I knew she must have spent an obscene amount of money on it. But, ungrateful (no pun intended) bitch that I am, I kept thinking, *A skateboard?*

"It's not to *ride*, you know," she explained, in a slightly offended tone. "It's a piece of *art.*"

"Oh, I know. Of course it's not to ride! I didn't think that!" I laughed nervously, adding, "I'd look pretty silly riding a skateboard at my age, wouldn't I?"

The rest of the evening had an unpleasant tension to it; I felt as if I'd committed an outrageous act of blasphemy by not being rhapsodically ecstatic about Dayna's gift. Dayna remained moody and I finally went home, once again using Jude as an excuse, and lugging my new skateboard under one arm.

I felt ashamed of my "disloyalty" to Jerry and the boys for exactly seven hours, six of which I'd been asleep. By the following day, I'd recovered and when I saw Dayna again, I managed to behave as though the previous night's awkwardness had never occurred. She had decided to put the uncomfortable scene behind us too, and we were immediately happy girl-friends again.

That same day, Dayna's car finally gave up the ghost and floated up to shitbox heaven. She mourned the loss stoically but I knew it pained her, particularly because of all those bumper stickers she wasn't able to peel off before the heap was towed away. Some of them, having been baked and frozen through many New England seasons, had become part of the car's skin, like old, faded tattoos.

Sympathetic lover that I was, I insisted on giving Dayna the spare key to my Honda, urging her to borrow it anytime she pleased until she found another vehicle within her budget.

She apparently took this generosity to mean, "Please take my car and cover it with as much Grateful Dead crap as you possibly can within a two-hour period," because the following Friday evening that's exactly what she did.

I stood outside a friend's house looking at my new Dead mobile. I'd been in a good mood all night, bragging about my sweet crazy girlfriend and her cute little obsession. Suddenly, I didn't think her obsession was so cute.

Standing on the sidewalk, I shouted things about a lack of respect for personal property.

I shouted, "Why didn't you just bolt a gigantic bong to the roof?"

I distinctly remember yelling, "Fuck my job! Now I can just sell magic mushrooms out of the trunk!"

Dayna leaned against the car, her arms folded across her chest, her faded blue eyes darkening to indigo. As calmly as possible, she tried to explain her side of the story. She said she'd been embarrassed to be seen in such a naked car; her friends had laughed at her. "And besides," she argued, "you said you *liked* all the stickers on *my* car!"

"Yeah," I bellowed, "as in, thank friggin' god it's not mine!"

The scene escalated from there, with Dayna ripping bumper stickers off the Honda and tossing the tattered remnants up into the air like psychedelic confetti. I went into pout mode and we drove back to her place in stony silence. Without a word, she got out of the car and slammed the door, taking her porch stairs two at a time. I sped away with a satisfying screech of rubber, already determined to not back down on this one. I knew I was right, dammit!

The whole weekend passed and I stood my ground. I didn't call her at all. I was quite pleased with myself as I walked through the thrift store doors Monday morning with an air of righteousness, feeling I had made my point.

And there was Dayna, in a Grateful Dead T-shirt featuring sunflowers, jeans held together with Grateful Dead patches and her trusty Peppermint Patty sandals. Her fiery hair was held back with a new cherry-wood clip, and the moment she saw me, she dazzled me with that damn smile. I felt my heart stutter. She looked like an acid-test angel, like the Good Witch of Woodstock.

We met each other in the middle of the sales floor, each of us full of apologies and regret, laughing at our moronic little tiff. I told her how much I'd missed her, not realizing it was true until the words had left my mouth. She confessed that she'd picked up the phone to call me a dozen times over the weekend.

I was relieved that we were okay. There was something truly intoxicating about this woman; I loved being in her presence and I thought that if to be with her, I had to deal with her being a card-carrying Deadhead, then so be it. What was wrong with me anyway? Why was I being so ridiculous about it? So she loved the Grateful Dead. So what! There were plenty of things

I loved that she didn't, and she wasn't freaking out on me about it, was she? I would just have to learn to live with her fanaticism; I would have to learn to compromise. That's what adults in adult relationships do, right? They compromise. And that's what I would do too.

I lived quite successfully by this philosophy for all of three weeks.

During that time, Dayna and I both found work in other fields and she moved to another city to be closer to her new job. She also managed to find an affordable car and though she relinquished the spare key to my Honda, she simply traded it for a key to my apartment. I was now working odd hours and because of Dayna's newly increased travel time, we decided it made sense for her to be able to come and go as she pleased.

I thought we had a perfect arrangement. Sometimes she would be there when I returned home and sometimes she wouldn't be, but it always seemed to work out exactly right. If I felt like seeing her, she would be there. If I just wanted to go home, veg out in front of the tube and not be bothered, she was nowhere to be found. It was like we were always telepathically on the same page. I couldn't have been happier.

One of the best parts of having Dayna at my house when I

wasn't there was that Jude had all the company she craved. She was a rather high-maintenance dog. Having been abused and rescued from the pound, she was skittish and afraid of her own shadow but always friendly and anxious to please.

Jude and Dayna bonded almost immediately, perhaps a little too much. I would come home from a long hard night, wanting nothing more than to crawl into my bed with my soft, snoring girlfriend and instead I would find the mutt in my place, head on my pillow, big brown eyes giving me the but-I'm-so-*comfortable* gaze.

The last night Dayna and I were together, Jude was giving me that same look, only this time from the sofa. I'd come in after midnight to find my two favorite girls in my living room, curled up and sharing a bowl of popcorn. Dayna was watching a rented movie and Jude was watching Dayna, or rather, she was watching Dayna's hand travel from the bowl to her mouth, over and over and over again. The dog barely even glanced at me when I came in.

"Some watchdog," I said, amused and thinking how sweet they looked snuggled into each other. "You two look so cozy, I actually hate to break it up." After watching them for a couple more seconds, I snapped my fingers and gave Jude the "get down" hand signal. She promptly ignored me. "Come on, Jude. Get down!" Still no response.

I frowned. She was usually such a good dog. "Jude!" I said firmly. "Down!"

Dayna paused the movie, looked at Jude and, with a mouth full of popcorn, said, "Down, Jerry!"

The dog whined, begging to stay, and Dayna repeated her command while I stood, completely dumbfounded. The dog jumped off the sofa and Dayna aimed the remote control at the VCR again.

"Whoa, whoa, whoa," I said, taking a step toward her. I tried to smile. Surely Dayna hadn't *meant* to call my dog *Jerry*. "You just called her Jerry."

Dayna giggled. "Isn't it cute? She's already used to it, I think."

Shaking my head to clear it, I knew I must have missed something. "What do you mean, she's *used* to it?"

"The name." Dayna looked at me as if she suspected I'd been sniffing glue. "I think she likes it."

"What are you talking about?" I demanded, suddenly feeling queasy. "You changed my dog's name?"

Apparently she sensed some displeasure on my part because

she abruptly sat up and tossed both the bowl and the remote aside. "Oh, god. Here we go."

"You changed my dog's name!" I began pacing my living room. "To *Jerry!*"

"Jesus, it's not that big of a deal! I just thought it would be cute!"

I stopped pacing long enough to glare at her. "Are you fucking crazy? You can't just change the name of a person's dog!"

Dayna sighed heavily and rolled her eyes. "Okay. Whatever."

"Didn't we discuss this, Dayna? Didn't we talk about having respect for each other's personal property?"

"An animal is *not* personal property!" she snapped. "Besides, maybe her name really *is* Jerry! Did you ever think of that? Why else would she respond to it so quickly? Huh? *Huh?*"

"Maybe because it's the only thing she ever hears out of your goddamned mouth!" I screamed. "She probably thinks you just call *everything* Jerry!"

We engaged in a stare down then, both of us enraged, with nostrils flaring.

"You know," she said finally. "You're *totally* overreacting."

It was at that moment that I realized this situation was not something I could ignore. I couldn't stand all this Grateful Dead nonsense for another single minute. I'd fooled myself into believing this girl's obsession was something I could live with as long as it meant I could be near her. That was all bullshit. I knew if I saw one more dancing bear, one more goddamned tuxedoed skeleton, I would scream off into the night and eventually be found drooling and chittering like a lab test monkey.

Naturally, the thought gave me the creeps.

I immediately told Dayna I couldn't continue seeing her, not even on a casual basis. To drive the point home I handed over the skateboard she'd given me, insisting I couldn't keep it knowing how much more it would be appreciated in her possession.

She handled the whole thing quite well. I suspect she had reservations about dating a non-Deadhead anyway. She called me a couple of times after that, but I was never home and I never returned those calls. I just never saw the point.

Still, I sometimes think about her and the strange trip we took together. I imagine she's out there somewhere, surrounding herself with tasteful shrines and priceless brassieres.

Punk Rock Sex God

Holly Wisniewski Case

Rick was the sexiest guy I'd ever seen, and from the first time I saw him I was determined to seduce him. I normally chose brains over looks when selecting my dates, but then again, I'd never before met a guy who so seemed to exude pheromones from every pore. When I set my sights on him, I placed the issue of intellect on the back burner. I assumed his smarts were merely overshadowed by his powerful sex appeal.

I first met Rick when he showed up at my friend's band practice on his motorcycle. He said he was the new singer, and I felt a wave of instant lust like I never had before. I was eighteen, but you must understand that this was no ordinary teenage crush.

19

There were a lot of things that made him worthy of my all-consuming passion. For one, he was twenty-seven years old, which equals worldly sophistication when you're just out of high school. He was not at all like most guys I knew; he was interested in politics and philosophy and punk music. He was a bad-boy cliché: He wore a black leather jacket with the anarchy symbol painted on the back in shoe polish, had tattoos on his muscular biceps and had a Mohawk with the tips of his hair dyed flame-red. His dark eyes were unusually piercing: When he looked at you, you felt that you had his total attention. He stared a lot. The constant staring intrigued me; I wanted to know what he was looking at or what deep thoughts were occupying his mind (his band mates told me it just meant that he was stoned). And the one thing about him that most turned me on was watching him perform. When he was onstage, he would close his eyes as though in ecstasy and sway his hips in a fluid, seductive way. It didn't matter that he was screaming rants about the government until he grew hoarse. His hips were singing a different song, like an invitation to his bed.

I wanted a relationship with him; I wasn't interested in a one-night stand. Lost in fantasyland, I constantly daydreamed about what life would be like once I was his girlfriend. I'd ride to the shows with him in the band's van, and all the other punk girls would be jealous of me when they saw me wearing his leather jacket. He could probably have his pick of the more hardcore punk girls at the shows, but he would fall in love with me because I was more sensitive. I was convinced that I was the only woman who could see through the tough-guy exterior; I believed that underneath it all, he was probably a shy guy who just needed love. I wrote poems about him in my notebook every night. Once he had a longer conversation with me, I knew he would realize that I was his soul mate. When I won him, our relationship would transcend the relationships I'd had with guys my own age, who all seemed shallow and immature. I was certain that Rick was more sophisticated, his punk world view surely the result of considerable life experience. And of course, since he was older, I imagined that he knew a lot about sex that the younger guys did not.

I started making sure I was in his path more often; I hung around backstage after shows. One night, the guys in the band and a large group of friends went to a park to hang out. When I arrived, Rick noticed that I didn't have any beer because I was underage, so we rode to the store on his motorcycle and he bought me a forty-ounce bottle of the cheapest beer available. I gripped his back as we rode and was nearly delirious from the excitement of touching him. We got back to the park, but it started raining. I invited him to sit in my car and finish our beers together, and he agreed. He put poorly recorded punk cassettes in my stereo without asking me. "You hear that? This is the most fuckin' awesome band," he said about each one. "Their lyrics are so right on, they really know what's goin' on!" I couldn't really understand the lyrics because the vocals were too fast and garbled; I liked the energy of the music but couldn't comment otherwise. I found that talking to him was a little less interesting than I'd hoped, so I drank faster. After a couple of hours, I was completely drunk and was able to steer the conversation to the topic of my all-consuming lust for him. He listened with an amused smirk on his face. "So," he said, "imagine you got me alone for an hour; tell me what you'd do to me." I didn't waste time with coyness or double-entendres. I told him that I wanted to taste him, to let him gently bite at my neck, to feel the sweat from his body mingled with mine. He continued to tease me. "What makes you think I bite? I don't think I'm scary," he said, chuckling. I told him that I saw intensity and passion in his eyes. And without even a hint of embarrassment, I told him about the poems I'd written about him and recited a few lines. To his credit, he did not laugh.

The night ended with me dropping him off at his parents' house and him saying that he would see me around sometime. He seemed neither offended by my admission of lust, nor particularly interested. I briefly entertained fears that I had made an ass of myself by being so forthcoming with my feelings, but I quickly pushed those thoughts out of my mind. He was a sex god, but I was worthy. This lack of response, of course, only fueled my belief that he was an enigma and drove me harder to seduce him.

Still, it didn't appear that the relationship was progressing at all. If it was a hot night when we sat around drinking in a group, he'd jokingly tell me to take off my shirt so I could cool down, but that wasn't exactly a step toward a relationship. It was taking longer for him to ask me out than I had expected. But he was still regularly coming over to hang out, which I took as a positive sign. He hadn't written me off yet, and I was going to make sure that he didn't. My friend Jen wanted to fix me up with one of her brother's friends; she said it would be good for me to get my mind off Rick and have fun with some other guys. I refused; I was not ready to give up.

Finally, in the middle of the hottest August in years, he called. It was the first time he'd ever called me on the phone. I was shocked when one of my roommates handed me the receiver and Rick's voice was on the other end.

"Hey babe," he said, his voice sounding even huskier and sexier over the line. He hesitated for a moment, and I could hear him exhaling cigarette smoke.

"What's up, Rick? Do you need to score some pot? 'Cause if you do, Dave's at work right now."

"No, no, that's not it. I . . . uh . . . was wondering if you wanted to, like, go out on a fuckin' date and stuff."

I was stunned into silence. At eighteen, I'd gone out with a few guys, but not one had ever formally asked me on a date. I fell even harder for Rick; a bad boy with a secret romantic side was my ultimate fantasy. "Where are we going?" I asked.

"Dude, that's a secret. I promise you'll like it, though." He let out a low laugh. I agreed to the date. He said he would pick me up in an hour.

When I got off the phone, I jumped around excitedly. I knew all along that I could make him want me! My roommate looked at me like I was insane. She hadn't particularly liked Rick since the night he mistook her bedroom closet for the bathroom and peed all over her clothes. I knew that she, too, would eventually be able to see his sensitive side and would learn to like him. Rick showed up almost three hours later with a case of cheap Black Label beer strapped to the back of his bike. He helped me strap on an aqua-green motorcycle helmet, making me think I'd wasted my time attempting to gel my hair into punky little spikes. I found it chivalrous that he'd brought a helmet for me, since he never used one himself. As he helped me climb onto the bike, he said, "Nice ass." I knew then that I had chosen well when I decided to wear my tightest black shorts. I still had absolutely no idea where we were going.

I rode on the back of the bike for what seemed like forever. I felt free, gliding into the open summer air, but I was nervous too. He finally brought me to a small clearing of beach at a state park. When we first arrived, a well of hope sprang up in me that he was creating a romantic scenario wherein we'd make love on the beach. But I didn't know that the state park had been virtually abandoned years ago, and the only visitors there were the pigeons. Nobody had bothered to clean up the discarded potato chip bags and empty beer cans from the previous summer, and the smell was pretty bad. I looked around at the veritable swamp in front of me and decided that there would be no naked romp on the beach, even if he wanted it. I started to wonder if this was really his idea of a great place for a date, or if he was testing me to see exactly how much I wanted him. We sat in the clearing, watching the sun go down and drinking our beer. Mosquitoes bit my legs, and my arms were scratched from sitting among scrubby, overgrown plants. The conversation was still somewhat awkward, despite the copious beer I'd consumed. He talked a lot about the "system"; today he focused on schools.

"You know, teachers are fuckin' oppressors, too," he said. "You learn what they tell you to learn, stuff you'll never use in the real world. They set up all the smart kids to get made fun of and egg on the jocks to be stupider."

I ignored the fact that Rick was making a point about intellect while using the word "stupider." "Yeah, I agree with that," I said. "It's true that they set up the smart kids to be targets of teasing from other kids. And I can't remember when the Civil War started, but I guarantee it's never been relevant to my life."

He agreed. He stood up, faced away from me and peed into the bushes. When he was finished, he remembered another point he found crucial about the tyranny of public school. "They make you sit there, and you, like, need to ask to take a piss. What's up with that? This is the US of fuckin' A, taking a piss is a Constitutional right."

I laughed more loudly than I intended. "Rick, I don't think taking a piss without having to ask permission is a Constitutional right."

"Well, fuck that," he replied. There was nothing more to be said.

Mercifully, he finally decided it was time to leave the beach. I was frustrated with the nature of our date so far. If he just dropped me off again and gave me more of that enigmatic no-reaction crap, I'd have to kick him. But that's not what he did. When we got to my place, I invited him to come in and he agreed. It was awkward making the transition from our usual conversational interaction to a sexual one. We sat around smoking for a few minutes, dropping the ashes in a Coke can. I started blowing smoke rings and he said, "I'd like to see what else you can do with that mouth." Once we got started, I was definitely not disappointed. His sexual experience was even greater than I'd expected. He took his time with me and left no inch of my body untouched. I thought, *Well, he's pretty stupid, but he can do some amazing things with those hands and lips.* Maybe I could overlook the fact that he wasn't a great conversationalist.

I didn't see or hear from him for two or three days after that. My roommate was highly unimpressed. "So," she taunted, "you finally got to sleep with your punk rock sex god, and now he isn't even calling. I guess punkers aren't any more considerate than other guys, huh? What an asshole." But I wasn't worried at all. Any time he came to mind, I just remembered seeing him with those dirty jeans off, and I was far too happy to worry about anything.

Sex soon became the central component to the relationship, indeed, pretty much the only component, so we planned to talk more and just hang out. "Hey, I was thinking today about how jobs suck the life out of us, man," he said. I had to roll my eyes; we'd had this conversation the last time we hung out together. "You go to work for some corporate asshole, who gives you, like, shit for pay, and meanwhile he's getting rich off your labor and driving a fuckin' BMW. The intellectuals of the world like me can't do anything except deliver pizza, but if you kiss the right person's ass you can be a goddamn CEO." And with that, he hit the table for emphasis and dropped his cigarette butt in the empty Boone's Farm wine bottle on the floor.

He looked at me and lifted an eyebrow as if to ask what I thought of his great contribution to the conversation. "Well," I began slowly, "I think being employed at all is kind of a prerequisite to becoming a CEO."

He gave me a dirty look and informed me, "Jobs are for

losers—no offense." He ranted on about the evils of corporate big shots spending their money on fancy houses and cars (sounding more than a little envious), but I was having trouble concentrating.

"I'm tired of watching all these bur-go-zee pigs getting it all. I want my fuckin' share of the pie!" he yelled.

"What kind of pigs?" I asked.

"Burgozee, you know, yuppie scum."

"Do you mean bourgeoisie?"

"What-the-fuck-ever. Who do you think you are, an English teacher or something?" He glared at me a little.

I'd finished all my beer, and his drumming on the table while talking was driving me nuts. I stared off, trying to send telepathic messages. *Shut up already. I already know what you think of the system. Stop tapping your fingers before I break them off.* Finally, I got up to leave. "Hey Rick, I think I'm gonna go home. It's been a long day and I need to get up early for work tomorrow."

He stopped tapping and moved in closer to me. "Hey baby," he said while nuzzling my neck, "I'm sorry I was talking about so much heavy shit. Let's see if we can play a bit and have some fun." He slid his hands smoothly down my legs, kissing my neck. I dropped my purse on the floor and gave in.

This, of course, happened again and again once he learned how to seduce me into staying around.

Sometime after he uttered the phrase "system keeping us down," I would start formulating my escape plan. Then, as though he had a sixth sense, when I was about to open my mouth to say goodbye, he would begin to kiss me and I would remember why I put up with him. As time went on, he got more sexually adventurous, and I was reluctant to kick him out, simply because I was dying to know what he wanted to do with me next.

After two or three months, I was really getting worried that there was absolutely nothing redeeming in our relationship besides the sex. One of his favorite activities was watching cartoons in the dark with me while eating Fruity Pebbles cereal. "Hey, didja know that any combination of colors of the Pebbles on your spoon always makes pink milk? Fuckin' awesome cereal! It's like magic or something," he said. He kept a chalk tally on the wall of how many cereal nuggets he could fit on a spoon at one time. "Dude, I think if I can get more than thirty Pebbles on the spoon, I could get into that record book—what the fuck's it called? Guinness?" I told him I doubted there was a cereal-crowding category in the *Guinness Book of World Records*, but he was not deterred. He just said, through a mouthful of cereal, "You don't support my dreams! You don't believe in me!" Maybe there was validity to his claim, so I resolved that the next time I saw him I would be open-minded and try to express genuine support for his pursuits. I did care about him, even if he wasn't the brightest guy in the world.

The next time he came over, my roommate let him in while I was taking a nap after having worked a late shift at the restaurant. I woke from my nap to a bizarre smell coming from the lower level of the house. I wandered downstairs and traced the putrid smell to the kitchen. "What the hell is that smell?" I asked loudly. Rick was stirring something in one of my saucepans on the stove. "It's Sudafed," he said. "I crushed it all up and now I'm boiling it down with some rubbing alcohol. I think it'll be like hash and give me a better high. It's gonna be fuckin' sweet."

I covered my nose, peeking in the pan at the bubbling red decongestant mixture. "What are you going to do with it?" I asked. He wasn't a hardcore drug addict; he didn't mess with needles. I couldn't imagine what he was planning. I didn't know you could get high on Sudafed in the first place. "Dude, I'm gonna smoke it in my bong," he said. He leaned over and gave me a kiss. "Of course I'm gonna share, babe."

My roommate was getting tired of hearing me complain about him all the time. "I told you he was a loser," she finally said.

"No, you didn't! Why didn't you warn me?"

"Come on, everyone warned you. You were just too blinded by lust to listen." I tried to protest, but I knew it was true. I vaguely remembered that a few people did indeed warn me, questioning whether or not I wanted to be with a guy who wasn't very bright.

The dilemma of whether or not the sex was great enough to outweigh the huge annoyance of conversing with him became much clearer the night we went out to dinner with some old friends of mine. We went to the only restaurant in town that charged more than ten dollars for an entrée; I figured this occasion called for a little more class. "Hey, Rick," I said. "This place is kind of fancy, so it would be really cool if you could dress up a bit. They might have a dress code." He muttered something about dress codes being part of a fascist plot, so I was nervous to see what he would do. He was totally stoned when he showed up for dinner. He must have found some money for real drugs because he reeked of pot. His blue jeans were ripped and had mud stains on the ankles. He was wearing the same torn, stained Black Flag T-shirt he'd been wearing when I last saw him two days earlier, and it didn't look or smell like he'd even taken it off since then. He sat at the table through the entire dinner, drumming on the salad plate with his utensils and not speaking to anyone. He didn't seem to notice the glares of everyone else in the restaurant. "Rick!" I hissed in a stage whisper. "Stop the drumming already!" He looked down sullenly, but then his eyes became fixated on the sleeve of his leather jacket. For at least fifteen minutes he stared very intently at his jacket sleeve, sometimes cocking his head to one direction and then the other, as though to appraise the jacket from different angles. Then he leaned his head closer to it. At first I thought he was going to pass out or fall asleep, but I was wrong. He put his head down an inch from his sleeve and inhaled very deeply, smelling it. He more loudly and deeply sniffed his sleeve several times, completely oblivious to the fact that everyone near us was staring at him. Nobody knew why he was doing it. He didn't seem to know either; it was as if he was in a trance.

After dinner Rick and I sat outside the restaurant smoking cigarettes, trying to decide what to do next. He put his hand on my thigh. "Hey babe, ya want me to come over and have some fun together?" he asked.

"No, I don't think so," I said sadly. The mystique had worn off. Somehow watching him sniff his jacket and imagining what it must smell like had been a real wake-up call. The best sex in the world wasn't worth another discussion about how "the system keeps us down" or the endless possible things he could smoke to get high. I wanted to have dates that required my brain more than they required alcohol. I realized what I was giving up sexually; it would be years before I'd have sex that good again. But the attempt to converse necessitated more effort than I could handle.

The day after our disastrous jacket-sniffing dinner date, I went to see him at his parents' house and told him the relationship was over. He looked genuinely forlorn and asked, "Why do women always do this to me?" For a moment, I almost felt bad. But after the breakup, I took solace in the fact that I wasn't the only woman who fell under his spell. He and the guys in the band moved on to Minneapolis a few years later and were modestly successful in the underground punk scene. I went to most of their shows in a three-state radius, and without fail some woman always pointed him out and spoke wistfully of how she had gone out with him but in the end, he was too stupid to tolerate. He was a legend, in more ways than one.

Don't Stop by and See Me Sometime

Antonia B. Johnston

I liken the "young, cute boy cycle" to a longer-lasting sort of PMS: You never have the clarity to see what's coming until after it's hit—even though it descends like clockwork, even though the symptoms are the same every time. You bitch out a few friends, throw red wine at your family members or coworkers, and then—blam!—you get your period. It's like waking from a deep slumber to a gun pointed at your head.

I think I started "seeing" ("dating" implies dates) guys about seven or eight years younger than I am shortly after my thirtieth birthday. Usually I find someone in the late fall so I can stay warm that winter. Or I hook up with someone in April because, like T. S. Eliot wrote, "April is the cruellest [*sic*] month."

These affairs, which stir my dull, gray roots (and not just the ones on my head), begin with a brief illusion of newfound youthfulness and a corresponding ego boost, and usually end well before Valentine's Day or my birthday in June. To be honest, in the interest of getting laid, I've inadvertently left a trail of beautiful-boy blood. Maybe I just like to see if I can get away with it. They say the conquest is a man's territory, but I enjoy it too—to hell with consequence.

Usually I plan for a one-night stand. There's an unspoken rule, though: The ones you want to see for more than one night don't want to see you again, and the ones you think you won't see again *do*. I never know until morning, when the guy asks for my number or just splits, whether I have been chosen to baby-sit for the next few months. It's getting harder not to feel like a mother, so why do I bother? Sex. The single guys my own age can barely get it up. Maybe it's because they tend to be drunks or junkies—just a theory. You can't come when you're on heroin because your body is already in an orgasmic state.

Anyway, there are myriad blessings and curses of the cute young guy. They're horny, like I am (you know what they say about women in their thirties), so it's a good libido match, but they ultimately disappoint. It's not their fault. Why should they know the number-one album of 1977? They were barely born. Or have any sense of responsibility? They're still battling separation anxiety from their mommies. How could they possibly understand or comprehend my rich and experience-filled life, with its incessant stream of weddings and baby showers? Why would they want to? I should know all this by now.

Still, even at this tender age, they should know that the unannounced stop-by is not an option. In college, my friends were always stopping by—we lived in dorms and homes we never locked. And even after college, before careers and romance monopolized our time, it seemed perfectly natural to stop by (preferably with a six-pack or some weed) at almost any hour.

But I've never liked to be the *receiver* of the stop-by. Especially from a lover. I'm territorial and controlling; my home is my sanctuary. If I lived in a cardboard box, I would still cherish and decorate my space.

And I'm very clear that with these horny youngsters, the stop-by is merely a less sophisticated form of the booty call—except it doesn't wait for my permission, or caller ID (how often I have wished for doorbell ID or those secret doorcams security guards use at office buildings). The stop-by doesn't wait for me to get dressed, put on makeup, empty the cat's litter box or do the dishes. The stop-by doesn't wait for me to hide my dildo or my pot. Yes, perhaps the horny enthusiasm and romantic spontaneity of the stop-by should flatter me, but it doesn't.

Which leads me to Joey. Once, I dated the son of a Mafioso. That wasn't the problem, that was my goal: With my predilection for Italian men, expensive taste in toiletries and general high-maintenance profile, I was bound eventually to desire to be a Mob wife, thinking it must be more interesting than merely being a Waspy, boozy housewife, like my mom. Hollywood movies didn't help.

I told my friends about the exciting future I envisioned, working the stereotype for all it was worth: He wouldn't want me to work and he'd buy me nice stuff. The sex and the food would be great, plus there would be lots of drama.

"That's ridiculous," my friend who had previously talked me out of entering the escort business insisted. "Don't you think it would be wrong to put your children in constant danger?"

It may be, too, that I am easily bored.

Still, I was sure I wanted him. I asked my friend, the owner of the coffee shop we both frequented, if he was available.

Reader's Digest

The Reader's Digest Association, Inc.

ACCESS NO.:

122659 1023 5426

	Annual Cover Price:	Gift Subscription Rate:	Annual Discount Savings Off Cover Price:
	$35.88	$27.98 Plus state tax, if any.	22%

COURTESY RATE:

12 issues/
$27.98

SAVINGS OFF COVER PRICE

22%

12/2798

PREFERRED GIFT DISCOUNT VOUCHER

Send my Reader's Digest Gift Subscription to:

NAME _____

ADDRESS _____ APT# _____

CITY _____ STATE _____ ZIP _____

Bill me $27.98 for 12 issues, plus state tax if applicable:

NAME _____

ADDRESS _____ APT# _____

CITY _____ STATE _____ ZIP _____

SEND NO MONEY NOW – WE'LL BILL YOU LATER.

22 % SAVINGS

N6DNSA01

BUSINESS REPLY MAIL

FIRST-CLASS MAIL   PERMIT NO 419   RED OAK IA

POSTAGE WILL BE PAID BY ADDRESSEE

Reader's
Digest

PO BOX 8064
RED OAK IOWA 51591-3064

"Yeah, but he's only twenty-four."

"Oh, that's okay," I said. I knew what I was doing. "Does he have a car?"

"He does, but I don't think he drove today," he said with a sneaky smile.

Did little Joey need a ride home? Sure he did. We stopped for a drink, as if it's a matter of course to get a drink when ostensibly just giving someone a lift home. When we got to his place, right away I noticed on his bookshelf a framed photo of him kissing a beautiful woman. *He could have the good sense to hide that*, I thought. I later found out it was a picture of him and his mother.

Okay, that's cool. At least he didn't hate his mother. (And she doesn't mean to call *every time* we're having sex, it just happens that way.) Joey wasn't stupid; in fact he was going to college because his dad did not under any circumstances want his son to enter "the business." Still, this meant certain odd things for Joey. Like lots of trips to their Key West getaway when things got too heavy for his family in New York. And lots of panicked calls from his mother.

Definitely, he was different than any boy I had dated—except for his huge ego, those come standard—but he had potential. He liked cats. He was loyal to his family, sensitive and musical. I was trying to be open-minded. So what if his musical tastes made me want to puke? Most people's taste in music makes me cringe, so that criterion had to go out the window.

And I was feeling pressure. Biological pressure. I started to have these delusions that Joey, who had just begun to experiment with sex and partners, would make me the last stop on his love train. Yeah right. Still, when we started doing it freestyle—without condoms—I worried, *What if?* I knew the answer: He wouldn't want it, and in all honesty, some part of me would. Not so much because he's "the one" but because of the incessant ticking. All the reminders of the limited life span of my thirty-three-year-old uterus were causing very uncharacteristic behavior on my part. It's funny how you start to want something just because you might not get it. To my surprise, something about Joey, whether real or imagined, really made me wish I could stop time for myself to let him catch up. In a bizarre twist of hope and dread, I would take a pregnancy test at the slightest tardiness of my period.

Then one day, I got a call. As usual, I checked my caller ID. It was Joey calling on his cell phone, an object that inspired serious reservations, even about him. My friends aren't cell-phone people. I wanted to be left alone and he'd been calling all day. I let the machine get it.

"Hey babe, I just left you a present by your front door. Run down and get it."

Shit. That meant he was calling from his SUV (another reservation-inspiring possession). He was out there somewhere. He knew I was home; he had seen my car. I was actually nervous. And I love presents. Guys never give me presents! Joey had given me another present the week before, Chanel #19! What a dirty trick. That bastard. He knew my curiosity would get the best of me. What if someone else got to my present first? What if it was jewelry? Like major, let's-have-babies jewelry? It was just sitting out there. But if I went to get it he'd be there at the door too, and then I'd be trapped and he'd know I'd been screening his calls all day. This was worse than a booty call or a stop-by, it was a booty call/stop-by combo with a bribery bonus.

I tried to calm down. If I could just see the front of the building from my apartment, I could tell if he was there and determine the shape of the present. I came up with an ingenious plan. I asked my neighbor to let me in his apartment to look out his window.

"What's the matter? You're shaking. Someone stalking you or something?"

"Sort of. Not really."

"Should I call the police?"

Oh *that* would be funny. "No no no, just let me look out your window."

The coast appeared to be clear. I couldn't see the present, but I didn't see Joey or his SUV either. I made a mad dash for the front door, barely poked my head out and grabbed my present, a single rose sitting idly on the step.

As soon as I got back up to my apartment, the phone rang. I felt his presence. He had parked outside and watched me. He thought a convenience-store rose wrapped in polka-dotted plastic guaranteed admittance and a thank-you fuck. I'd show him and his mama's boy, suburban sense of entitlement otherwise. I may have been cornered, but I could still ignore the phone.

I'd like to envision myself as a somewhat nicer person, sitting on the stoop with him to explain, patiently taking his hand in mine and patting his knee. Or running my fingers through his thick hair and tenderly resting my hand on his even softer cheek. "You know, Joey," I'd explain like some teacher in an after-school special, "as much as I like you, dropping by unannounced is simply inappropriate."

Still, I wouldn't let him in. I'd explain how, now that he had invaded my time and space in such a profound way, that he would have to go home and see me another time. This would really hit home: no nookie for the unacceptable stop-by, with or without a rose. But "inappropriate" is one of my most hated words, and this motherly tone was something I was trying to move away from. My abounding desire to care for and nurture someone conflicted with my pride and independence. This is where I always get confused as to the difference between being a mother and a lover. And some guys want you to be their mommy *and* their whore. It's very confusing.

But Joey thought he was helping with his stop-by. He thought he was being romantic. He called five more times. He wasn't going to give up. He knew I was home. And the thing was, I had just lost my job. So under these special circumstances, I finally let him in and took him to bed. I figured the sooner we did it, the sooner I could get him to leave, forgetting that a lovemaking session with Joey was a two-hour, six-orgasm commitment.

Two hours later, Joey was noodling on my guitar. As if I'd be impressed. This goes under "turnoffs" in my *Playboy* question-naire. I don't go to *men's* houses and just start playing *their* instruments as if I am some virtuoso noodler. Noodling annoys. Every single guy I have ever brought home does this, even if they can't play. It certainly seems like all those guitar-as-penis-extension theorists are on to something.

My annoyance turned to an urge to destroy as Joey followed me around my apartment, trying to tackle me as I dressed for an event for which I was two hours late. The thing that got me was he couldn't even see that I was annoyed. It was then I knew the stop-bys would never cease. Mad enough now for clarity, I catalogued his other, rather glaring faults. There was his fashion sense: the proudly tacky Liberace-inspired dress shirt with the rhinestone buttons, and later, the cowboy hat, ten times bigger than his little head. His bad poetry was full of Bukowski-esque machismo. Especially frightening, and the subject of much teasing and speculation, was a collage on his bedroom wall of pictures of blond models he had cut from fashion magazines. Then there was the time he'd handed me his cell phone while driving so I could "meet" his mother (who still sent the family's maid for his laundry).

That "relationship" ended the next time I saw him. Publicly. The next day, he quit his job and moved back in with his parents. Of course, once it was over, I realized I had let myself overlook *many* glaring mismatches, blinded as I was by maternal urges and a sex drive in high gear.

I learned.

I might like to have a baby, but I don't need to sleep with one.

The Man Who Mistook His Hat for His Date

Elizabeth Schilling

Would you like to dance?"

The question so flatters you that you almost fall out of your chair. It is the evening of your birthday, you're freshly out of a relationship, and this man finds you attractive enough to ask you to dance.

Despite your profound disability where social dancing is concerned, you accompany him to the dance floor. You follow his lead gamely, stepping on his feet only twice. He wears an orangey-yellow sweater, well-worn jeans and boots. He also wears a pea-green fedora and a beard. Beards aren't one of your weaknesses—not since the one worn by an ex-lover who could wear a beard without looking like Freud. Your dance partner says hoarsely through his Freudlike beard, "I'm a psychiatrist and an epidemiologist. I consider myself a scholar of Elizabethan poetry as well. I attended Harvard . . . " A swoop of violin music drowns the rest.

"Is an epidemiologist a skin doctor?" you ask at the bottom of a musical swell. Under the hat his forehead furrows, and his eyes express pity. "Epidemiology is the study of epidemics." He launches into a lengthy monologue you can barely hear, on violence and his research. Over the next hour you dance and sit out dances with him and find out more about violence than you ever thought to. As you shrug on your coat at the end of the evening, he says, "I'd like to take you to dinner." He has nice eyes, so you say yes.

Date One

At 7:00 P.M. he is to whisk you to the best Japanese restaurant in the city—that's what he's promised over the phone. You scuttle home from work, bathe, dress in your most chic ensemble, and by 6:55 look fabulous. Then you sit down to wait for his arrival.

And wait. At 7:10 you begin to wonder if he'll show. At 7:15 the phone rings. Community Services for the Blind wants your old clothes and household items. At 7:25 you are furiously planning what to say if he calls with a lame excuse—or worse, doesn't call or show up—when there's a knock at the door. You open it. He enters in his hat, the same saffron sweater and the same pair of ratty jeans he wore the night you met him. He does not offer a word of explanation for his lateness; nonplussed, you follow him down the stairs and out to his car. His wallet juts precariously out of a hole at the bottom of his jeans pocket.

At the restaurant he suggests the salmon teriyaki. The sashimi plate tempts you, but as the gracious, good-sport date, you let him order the salmon for you. He orders sake and then the sashimi plate for himself. While the waitress is there, he explains: "Sashimi is raw fish. So, tell me something personal about yourself."

"Like what?"

He takes off his hat and lays it on the bench seat next to himself. His side hairs are clipped short, but long strands of hair combed from left to right cover the bald spot on the crown of his head. "Oh, anything," he says, flourishing his hand. "Well, since you can't think of anything, I'll tell you something

about myself. I flew to Cape Barrow to see the aurora borealis."
He launches into a lengthy tale of his travels by bush plane to
a small town on the Arctic Circle. With a great show of forced
laughter, he says, "I've never seen so much pornography in my
life. Stacks of it."

"So there weren't any women there."

"It's an oil rig. Of course there weren't any women."

"But I thought you went to a town. Cape Barrow."

"Oh, well. Yes. Later I went to the oil rig to see the lights.
Well then, what about something personal?"

As a prelude to your story, you ask, "Are you a spiritual
person?"

"Everybody is spiritual."

"Are you religious?"

"No. I'm an atheist."

"So you don't believe in anything?"

"No." He sneers out his noes! "Some atheists do believe that
a god for atheists exists . . . " You wonder at this statement. "But
I had an experience in my younger years. It was the first time I
was in love. When I asked her to marry me, she said she would
if I would accept Jesus Christ as my savior."

"She was a fundamentalist Christian?"

"Born-again. She'd never told me because she was afraid that I would break up with her. So I said I would try to accept Jesus Christ as my savior. And I prayed for a sign. But none came, so we went our separate ways. Are you going to eat the rest of your salmon?" Without waiting for an answer, he hefts the salmon with his fingers from your plate into his mouth. Then he launches into a story about a compulsive hand washer for whom he is trying to schedule surgery in order to cut out, as he puts it, a smallish part of the man's brain. "You have no idea how hard it is to set up something like that," he says mournfully.

When the check comes in its little portfolio, he picks it up, scrutinizes it and shuffles bills in and out of his wallet. You're not sure what it means. Finally, after shuffling the bills around for a while, he lays out three twenties with the check and puts them in the little portfolio. Then: "Here, let me cover for you."

"Thank you." It dawns on you that he expected you to share the bill! You think back—he asked you to dinner, which seemed to imply that he would pay. You don't know what to think, and indeed don't have time for he is almost out the restaurant door. Together you walk to his car. He is bareheaded. You say, "Didn't you have a hat?" Wordlessly, he clumps back to the restaurant, leaving you standing by the locked passenger door in the rain.

From the constrained silence on the drive home, it seems this date has not been a success on either side. You feel a little sorry. You say, mostly to break the silence, "The night we met was my birthday."

"How old are you?"

"Thirty-five."

By his reaction, you know he thought you were younger. "And you?"

He hesitates. "I'll be thirty-five in January." A curious power-balance shift in your favor happens right then. He seems less arrogant. You wonder if the oddness of the evening was due to first-date jitters on both sides.

DATE TWO

For the next date, he invites you to a puppet show. You scramble home on the bus, gulp down dinner, hastily shower and dress in order to be ready by 7:00 P.M. Then you wait. You feel exhausted from hurrying and decide thereafter to make dates for later in the evening. And still you wait. At 7:30 he calls to say he is running late and that you'll have to meet him at the theater.

At the theater you amble around the foyer for half an hour

or so, looking at puppets hanging behind enclosed glass, reading the program a couple of times. He finally appears—in the saffron sweater, the same jeans and his hat. With a hangdog expression, he hands you a ticket. Then he stalks off to the men's room. You wait some more.

When he walks out of the men's room, a very long stream of toilet paper trails from his shoe. You watch in stunned fascination as he comes toward you. "Shall we sit down?" he asks. You follow him up the stairs and watch the toilet paper slide over the stairs after him like a comet tail. Is it his condescension toward you that makes you unable to say, "You have toilet paper on your shoe," or are you bewitched into silence by giddy and dangerous amusement? He discovers the toilet paper just as he arrives in full sight of the audience. He wipes his shoe over and over again on the carpet in front of everyone.

Despite the children sitting behind him, he keeps his hat on. The hat is a brownish pea-green with a band. "Ha, ha, ha." Your new friend lets out a deep bellowing bark of a laugh. You remember your best friend's injunction to give the man a chance—your best friend thinks you are a tiny bit too judgmental toward men. So you ask him to take off his hat, which he does after you explain why. Which perhaps explains why you agree, after the show, to meet him at the lake for a late-night walk. He's not so unreasonable. You wave at each other before you both set off *at the same time* for the lake.

You arrive first in the rainy October night and wait. You wait for ten minutes in the dark deserted parking lot. You begin to feel some of the same irritation that led you to break off your last relationship, and you decide to be kind and gentle. Finally he drives up. As you set off around the lake, he launches into a wrenching analysis of his emotionally unstable mother and why he felt abandoned by her. By the end of the story, which coincides nicely with the end of the walk, you feel completely wrung out. He asks, "Why such a somber look? Perhaps you need some tea. Let's go over there." He points to distant lights across a dark field. You follow him across the lawn under the trees in the rain.

"The grass is awfully wet," he says.

"There's a walk over there." You point past the gymnasium.

"No, no. That's not what I mean." He hands you the umbrella and bends over. To your absolute chagrin and mortification, he starts to lift you!

"No, please don't do this."

"Oh, come on."

"No, really, I . . . " Up you go into his arms. You have no choice but to hold on. He takes one unsteady step after another in the muddy grass. As he grunts and staggers beneath your weight, you feel yourself slipping from his arms. "Put me down. Please. I'm too heavy."

"You're not heavy," he says in a hurt voice, at last allowing you to slip out of his arms to the ground.

In the café, once you're settled with tea, he asks, "Why haven't you gotten married and had children?"

"I wasn't ready to. There's been too much else that I wanted to do. What about you?"

"I was married, once."

"For how long?" you ask. You're actually thinking, *For how long do I have to sit here?*

"Not long," he says lugubriously. He furrows his brows under his hat. "I no longer have any money because I spent it all on analysis in order to save the marriage. My wife was emotionally unstable."

"Really." You're thinking about the fiasco of the born-again fiancée. "What attracted you to her in the first place?"

"Her emotional transparency."

"What attracted you to your fiancée?"

"Well, *her* emotional transparency."

You don't ask him what attracted him to you.

DATE THREE

Reports come from your closest friends that they have seen and heard him interviewed on television and radio about violence, his field of specialty. He looks nice on TV. On the radio he sounds a little arrogant but very knowledgeable. Doubting your own perceptions, trusting your friends' instead, and to pay him back for the two times he's taken you out, you invite him to lunch and an exhibit of Rodin sketches and bronzes.

He gives you a complicated set of directions to his place. After getting lost a couple of times, you park in front of his building, a decrepit mansion, and pick your way up the stairs to his apartment on the top floor. Through a window in the door, you see rooms with paper-strewn floors, a minimum of furniture, and counters stacked with dirty dishes and pans—in short, chaos. Your heart sinks. You know by how empty it feels that he is not at home. You knock tentatively on the door. Then down the stairs you creep, feeling relieved.

When you reach the street, you see him driving over the crest of the hill toward you. He parks his car, which has a cracked windshield, half on the curb. He gets out, and guess what he's wearing—the jeans, the saffron sweater and the *hat!* He's carrying a bundle of wood and a bag of groceries. "Hello," you say. He shoves the grocery bag into your arms. You trudge behind him up the stairs, eyes level with the torn jeans pocket.

Littered with candy wrappers and academic papers, a futon sprawls in front of the wood stove. A table and chair are the only furniture. From the table, a huge orange cat eyes you. The psychiatrist points to a pot on the stove. "I made spaghetti last night. I can heat it up."

"No, really, but thanks." You put your hand out to pet the cat, and he bites you!

"Did he scratch you?" The psychiatrist pets your hand, jabbing his fingers into your breast. "Such tender skin," he murmurs.

"Gosh, we better get going," you say.

Over lunch at an upscale deli, he tells you the story about his ex-wife, whom he courted for three years. A week after the wedding he discovered she was, as he puts it, a Nazi. As he's relaying this, he sticks his thumb, smeared with mayonnaise, into his mouth to the hand joint. He does the same with his index finger. How could a man trained in observing detail court a woman for three years without discovering her anti-Semitism? How could he fall in love with another woman without discovering her fundamentalist Christianity? And how could he have such appallingly bad table manners?

You're still pondering these questions as you drive to the museum. Which trait will he discover in you that places you in the category of emotionally unstable—perhaps your compulsive curiosity? You laugh a little to yourself, and meanwhile drive along a line of parked cars in which there is one perfect-sized space. Yea! You stop next to the car in front of it, saying, "What a great space."

He says, "If you park here, you'll get towed."

"I don't see any signs." You back in.

Twisting his head around, he says, "Oh, yes, of course, you can park *here.*" He had thought you were going to double-park your car! You can only look at him.

In the gallery, you move from sculpture to sketch, admiring the beautiful lines of Rodin's work. The psychiatrist follows. Occasionally he touches you and puts his arm around you. You stand in front of a piece and watch in the glass's reflection as he walks up very close behind you. He is a much larger man than you realized. He stands close to you without touching you. You suddenly start to cough and can't stop. You cough, and cough, and cough. You finally have to leave the gallery. So much for that moment pregnant with eroticism. But it's time to leave anyway.

On the way to your car, a man speaking a mix of Russian and English stops you. You ask, "What? Do you need money?" The man says, *"Nyet."* Smiling proudly, he reveals a video camera under his coat to prove that he is not asking for money. He smells of alcohol. The psychiatrist has taken up a position some ten feet away. The foreigner, you finally understand, is having trouble with his rental car. He points to a white Taurus with flashing emergency lights. Behind the wheel, his friend smiles and waves. They need someone to phone the rental agency.

"Do you know where a phone booth is?"

The psychiatrist says impatiently, "He's a drunk. Oh, come on. He can take care of himself." He pulls you away. From the safety of the car, the psychiatrist chuckles, "There he goes," as the Russian runs after a pedestrian in the crosswalk.

You drive the psychiatrist home. He asks, "Would you like to come upstairs and have tea?"

"No," you say. "I don't feel well. I have to go home."

He says, "You could lie down here." He leans over to kiss you.

"I have germs," you say, backing off.

• • •

DATE FOUR

You're going on a fourth date. You repeat this to yourself in disbelief. He said he needs to get out and go hiking. You love hiking. That's why you agreed. No, that's not why. Why are you going? Some aberration in your character?

He's supposed to drive but calls up to say you have to. "I was trying to figure out a billboard and ran into the car ahead of me." He's smashed the front of his car because he was curious about a billboard. There's an object lesson here.

When he gets into your car, he offers to drive. You politely decline. He directs you to stop at the police station downtown so he can pick up an accident report. This takes forty-five minutes because he did not find out where he needed to go. But finally, you're on the freeway, driving to Camano and Whidbey Islands to eat lunch and to hike.

As you drive through the rain, a motorcyclist cloaked in a long coat and helmet passes by. The psychiatrist says, "Interesting fellows, those motorcyclists. I've always thought them rather feminine . . . " You look at him. "Because they tend to be emotionally histrionic and are very interested in clothing styles." You ignore the antiquated remark equating emotional histrionics with the feminine. Instead, you ask, "How is an interest in style feminine?" With an airy gesture of his hand, he says, "Oh, you know, they wear long coats and tattoos." He's wearing his usual ensemble. You let it go.

You take the turnoff for the island bridge. He's talking about how his emotionally unstable female supervisor at the clinic has it in for him. Rain falls steadily. You ask, "Did you bring rain gear?" He looks blank for a moment, then says, "No. Hmm, the restaurant is outdoor seating. I suppose we can sit in the car."

"It's a drive-up?"

Actually, it's a small seafood stand of white painted clapboard. A sign says, Closed for Season. He scratches his head. You're afraid that any moment you're going to become emotionally unstable. "Do you have any other ideas?"

He doesn't. The only place you know about is thirty minutes away, a rustic inn set off from the road on an inlet. So that is where you find yourself eating lunch on this cold early November day. Rain pounds against the windows and roof as the psychiatrist describes how his last supervisor tried to steal his research. In the ensuing brouhaha, both men lost their jobs. "The real story will never be known," he says mournfully.

Beneath the sound of his whiny story, you think back to the Christmas Eve you had dinner here with a lover and a close friend. After dinner you drank dark aromatic wine in front of a lovely fire until it was time to retire to the rooms above. Something in your lovely memory, juxtaposed with his whiny stories, prompts compassion for this sad man. "Look," you say. "It's stopped raining. Let's go hiking while it's still light." He knows of a park twenty-five miles south, where there's still old-growth forest. That's where you go.

A short hike down a well-maintained path takes you to the shore, where the tide is pounding toward cliffs. There's barely a safe path now. You shake your head. "We can't hike here with the tide coming in."

"We don't know for certain it's coming in," he says as he scrambles down to the beach. You can see it now, the two of you scrambling for dear life amid sea foam and the cliff face. "No," you say. You climb back up the hill to the car. He follows.

At the car, you unlock the car door. Wind flaps his overlay of hair into a bizarre configuration. "Where's your hat?" you ask, and immediately wish you had not. "I must have left it at the restaurant," he says. "But we can drive back for it."

Twenty-five miles you drive in the rain and silent dusk back to the inn. While he collects his hat, the windshield wiper goes back and forth eighty-seven times. With that hangdog expression, he gets into the car and puts his hat on the floor. No apology. No apparent awareness of the effects of his behavior. You drive back the way you have just come plus some miles to the ferry. Over your silence he condemns his emotionally unstable fundamentalist Christian sister for living in some backwater Idaho town and home schooling his nieces and nephews; he talks about his emotionally unstable supervisor's vendetta against him; and he talks about how he's finally got the surgery set up so the compulsive hand washer can have part of his brain surgically and permanently removed.

Without a single shred of compulsive curiosity left, you stop in front of his house in this silent night. His fumbling kiss, his promise to call you—all of that, then you drive up the street toward the crest of the hill. A look in the rearview mirror shows him standing in the middle of the road, watching after you, hatless. It's on the passenger side floor. You think to go back, but cry aloud, "No!"

The hat will make a lovely flame.

Oh Henry

Lauren Dockett

T he first time that Henry* and I got together he had a bad
case of gas. It was just one of those things, and really, it's rather
grade-school of me now even to point it out. We were in college at the time, and we were eating far too much hummus.
Vegetarian vapors, I divined back then, really don't smell any
better than the meaty variety. In fact, I myself could've flat-
tened a few flowers on the way to the party. But I was definitely free and clear when it came time for mashing with
Henry. He, on the other hand, was releasing Pepé Le Pew

---

*The names in this story have been changed to protect the countless parties
involved and the new fiancée. Good luck, honey.

clouds with unbridled gusto and pretending nothing was wrong. Instead, there was the surreptitious slipping of his tongue against my palate, the smashing of my nose into his cheek and attempts at various bolder moves made to deflect my attention from the enveloping fumes.

Usually I fall into hysterical snorting fits whenever anyone performs a bodily function in my presence. But Henry was trying so hard that night to deny his that I had to respect the effort. Maybe if it had been a different setting. If the summer moon hadn't silvered the dark, dancing edges of the palm trees. If school wasn't almost over for me, and Henry hadn't eyed me with such woozy longing just before we started in—as if . . . if I could just wait a second, he would take our lust and fashion hot wings that would raise us above the thick southern air and past the sad partings into forever. If things had been different, maybe I'd have paid more attention to the farting.

But I was awash in Henry's mouth. The cushiony push in his wide, rock-star lips. The pooling sweet water back by his molars. I am a sucker for mouths that never dry up and are able to pull off gentle, heated, pleasantly juicy kisses at a moment's notice. And Henry, even under gassy duress, had such a mouth. It was for the extended promise of that good mouth that I launched, that very first night, my practice of puckering up for Henry, taking shallow breaths and overlooking most everything he did.

The kind of guy your parents love only because they can no longer smell sex, Henry emanated sex. Granted, if you missed this, you could get dazzled by his odd exuberance, his überspiritual smarts, his preternaturally long eyelashes and his David Cassidy hair. I had known about Henry from the very first day I arrived at college. Scruffily attractive, he was one of the few guys in our small school of misfits who oozed anything close to charisma. By the time our first night together arrived, Henry had already slept with most of my friends.

It was another night, four years later and thousands of miles away from our gassy beginnings, when Henry's killer charisma finally backfired. We were a couple by then, living in San Francisco, and Henry was engaged in his weekly pub crawling mission, this time with our college buddy John. A beneficiary of the inner circle status bestowed on all who had attended our tiny school, John had recently moved in with us. He was a nervous but sweet stoner, a guy perpetually caught between a desire to master obscure physics equations and the pipe. When I woke up, it was to the muffled sound of John's voice from the living room. The two had been drinking, as usual, and had come home at 4 A.M. They were staying out in the living room, which meant only one thing: The night had not lived up to the amount of booze they'd consumed, and they were on to a new plan. Ours was a long apartment and I couldn't shout down the hall. So I got up to tell them it was a lost cause and drag Henry into bed.

Henry had been a boozer for as long as I'd known him. He lived alone during college, in a dilapidated house choked by tropical vines a short ride from our Gulf Coast campus. The place leaned like a shipwreck, and we visitors were always careful where we set down our drink bottles. It was a natural party destination, but Henry was careful not to let it become a crash pad. The man required his privacy. Over the years I'd watched him run out of ways to count the number of women he'd slept with in that house. It's funny to me now, my willingness to believe that upon his graduation Henry was fuming only for me. He had told me he was. Said we were fated to be together, and in a nice piece of romantic chivalry, moved himself across the country and onto my San Francisco doorstep, after only one short little venture into my pants.

Although passionate about the newly formed us, Henry was

a rather passive soul when he came to town. He was surprisingly willing to put up with my dawning bisexuality, for example, and assured me that if I played with the girls for a while, he'd be content to wait. Though I was initially distrustful of Henry's flexibility, in the end I was awed and flattered by it. I told myself that finding someone with the kind of love drive Henry possessed is a precious thing. It's a feat when you're looking and a dizzyingly undeniable gift when you're not. It was all it took back then to get me to turn my back on the girls, and relax into monogamy with Henry.

In all of our years together, this love drive of Henry's almost never faltered. Unfortunately, his other drives also stayed intact. That night he and John were out in the living room, I padded in my socks down our dark hallway, unable to hear the two of them talking, but able to make out the sounds of lousy jazz and moaning—the familiar refrain of Henry's porn. The closer I got to rounding the corner into the living room, the louder the moaning became, until I expected to face two straight men embarrassed to be sitting together in the same dark room with that racket.

Henry's predilection for porn was a small thing in my mind, an eccentricity that I'd have felt patrician objecting to, and something that was easily outdone by his pristine tending of our love life. Henry wrote me regular poetry and countless heartfelt love letters. He tossed incense sticks and dried flower petals in his envelopes. The paper always arrived dusty and stained. These were the smudges of passion. Henry liked to set a mood. He listened to Dead Can Dance and Tangerine Dream. When we moved in together, we got a cat and a futon for the floor. It soon became a house of heavy petting and exotic smells, where tapestries were draped over every conceivable surface and coming home always felt like trading in stale workaday stresses for the unbidden possibilities of an opium den.

A habit of removing our shoes at the front door had become entrenched over the years, and when I came to the end of the hall that night, still groggily wiping the sleep from my eyes, the first things I saw were Henry's grimy socks. He was lying on his side and his shoeless feet were dancing slowly off the end of the futon, as if he were deeply asleep and dreaming of a tricycle ride. His jeans were bagging a bit down there at his ankles, and my eyes followed their thread, until there, where Henry's lap should have been all on its own, was a head instead.

Over the years, my personal feeling had been that Henry's own head was absurdly dominated by his eyes. Henry had very big eyes. Big and blue like a perfectly limpid pool should be. Every time he blinked, a new lash tumbled and stuck to his flawless skin, where I plucked it and blew—wondering how I managed to hook and then fall for such a smoothie, and wishing that the strange sensation of doom he evoked in me would sail as easily away. Henry knew privately that despite the eyes, he had a lot to compensate for, and so he made good strong efforts to be endearing. He would bury his face in my lap on Saturday mornings, lamenting his previous night's drunken leering. I, rarely present for these nights, took it upon myself to convince him of his innocence. I thought Henry's confessions were sweet, and a sign of burgeoning ethics. Henry might have attracted women to him, I reasoned, but how could I fault him for that? Besides, the love he had coaxed in me was by then overcoming any early suspicions. As time wore on, Henry appeared utterly faithful. He had become a keeper. My mother, eager for me to settle down and smitten with Henry herself, was ecstatic.

John's head, his mouth stuffed full of Henry's cock, was grinding up and down like a carousel stallion. Henry's head was also weirdly affixed to John's lap, bobbing out its own enthusiastic rhythm. And as I stood above them, my hand inches away from the light switch, I was momentarily fascinated by the way they looked like some perverted, fleshly Escher prototype, fixed in the quiet gurgling strangeness of their sixty-nine.

It's amazing where your mind will go in times of shock. Mine rewound to a still fall night a few months before, when we tried to get our money's worth out of an high-season Yosemite cabin. After a particularly loving exchange, I snuggled under Henry's long body and asked him about the future. His blue eyes clouded and paled above me, and the piney comfort of the tight cabin walls went cold and claustrophobic in the ensuing silence. I remembered shifting my gaze to the gnarled boughs that made up the ceiling, suddenly aware of my obligation to stifle a scream when in a national park. When Henry rolled off me and started mumbling something about the welcome unpredictability of youth and the stifling formula of marriage, my mind went cottony. *I don't particularly want to march down the aisle myself,* I thought, as we made the quiet morning drive back home, but I did know that I wanted to be Henry's everything. His salvation. The rocking soundtrack to his life. The very last stop on his Babes-of-My-Youth Express.

Like so many of the wasted, revelatory occurrences in my

young life, the thing that haunts me now about walking in on
Henry and John is my lack of ninja action. I still cannot believe
the gods of foresight marionetted me into ballet class for all
those years without once stopping at the kung fu studio, even
when they damn well knew that Henry and the futon were in
the cards. Why didn't I at least flip the light switch and watch
the two of them scurry to the corners like exposed vermin?
Why not turn to the Ginsu knives behind me on the kitchen
counter and perform a little avenger's surgery right then and
there? Why, unlike all those women making license plates in
far-flung county prisons, did I not seize the moment?

Henry was not gay, just someone who liked sex. He
liked it so much and so often that given the right liquor
and tensions, many of his friends would do. Henry kept
his conquests to himself, just as I snuck back down
through the hall and kept what I'd seen to myself for two
daunting weeks. I don't really know why I held back.
Part of me wanted to watch him decay under the strain of
the lying and cheating. See the guilt eat him alive, white hairs
poke out of his youthful face, spittle dry and cake in the corners of his mouth until one day he just collapsed under the

strain of my righteousness: a prostrate, babbling babe with flagellation and eternal devotion on his mind.

But Henry seemed to be doing just fine. In fact, he looked great. Like a boy with a nice fat secret usually looks. Happy with his bad self. On top of his game.

When I finally cornered him in our basement and made him confess, Henry stared at me for a good long time. He offered no apologies, just some excuses and that tired line about how it wasn't me, but him. When I pushed him to tell me *what* was him, he actually threw up his hands and exclaimed, "I want my freedom!"

The need for emancipation is understandable to all who have been in a relationship for any length of time. I understood it. Henry got his. I believe in giving people their freedom. What I find is that telling others the truth is also freeing. In fact, I recommend telling as many people as possible.

Henry preferred to keep this particular story to himself. He quietly helped me pack my bags and, as I walked the hallway for the last time, treaded behind and grabbed me for a final hug at the door. He held on tight and hard and I swear, somewhere behind the sad moans and whispered sweetnesses, I heard the high-pitched whine of slowly escaping gas. When I finally extricated myself from Henry's long lover's arms and stepped out into the street, it was to a white-bright sun and chilly morning air. The cold sent a blast of crisp cleanness into my lungs, and I started off mildly entranced by these slicing new breaths and the smell, somewhere around the block, of something really, really good.

Go to Your Room

Judy Campbell

When I was twenty, I moved to Iowa City to start my freshman year of college at the University. At the time I wanted to be a writer, and I had been told that they had a famous program for that. I applied and was accepted. Without ever wondering why they hadn't asked for any actual writing samples or even an essay, I was flattered to get in and decided to attend. However, when I arrived in Iowa I discovered that the program was for graduate students only, and unless I found a new passion for animal husbandry I really had no business being there. I found myself living in a huge pink dorm filled with thousands of eighteen-year-old Iowans, liberated for the first time in their lives to vomit wherever they might choose.

I, as I liked to remind myself, had been out of high school for two years. One of those I spent on my own, in Africa, the other in New York. I had worked since I was thirteen. I had lived in Asia. Twice. Henry Rollins had hit me over the head with a microphone. I had attended a fourteen-day, silent Buddhist meditation. I once walked across the country on a peace march; I had worked as a bricklayer and in a bowling alley; I had inhabited the body of a cheetah while on acid; I liked the taste of sea urchin; and I had never, ever owned a can of Aqua Net. In short, I judged myself entirely too world weary, impossibly sophisticated and yet charmingly down home for anything dorm life could offer. In search of an atmosphere more suited to my rather complex sensibilities, I found myself spending all of my time drinking Pabst in a musty basement bar with a bunch of underemployed forty-year-olds. That's where I discovered my boyfriend.

Paul was thirty and, in the beginning of our relationship, his most attractive traits were his confidence, knowledge of local fauna and the paper sack of cocaine he always carried around.

That sack of cocaine introduced us. I was at the bar, ordering a drink, working on my, "I'm over twenty-one" grimace—a kind of pouty, scrunched-up look based on the premise that wizened twenty-five-year-olds were much uglier than cute, fresh twenty-year-olds. Ergo, the uglier I could make myself look, the older I seemed. Paul was sitting on the stool next to me. He had shiny, black hair pulled back in a short pony tail. His skin was patchy and a few different colors. His eyes were too small, his lips too big and he had extra pouches of skin under his chin but when he looked at me his eyelids drooped until his long curled lashes seemed to rest on his cheek. He considered me calmly under veiled eyes for a long time. I wasn't used to being looked at for just standing there, without breaking into some kind of vaudeville routine. His ugliness looked so good on him. It was a crazy confidence, as if he had so much going for him that being attractive as well would just be too unfair to the rest of us. I waited while he watched me, wanting desperately for him to approve of me. Without breaking his gaze he reached under the bar, into his backpack, took out the brown paper sack, and put it in my hand. It had a soft, pleasing weight that molded itself to my palm. Take this into the bathroom, he said, and keep as much as you like.

Paul was no small time dealer. No bouncing on the balls of his feet in some alley. No knocks in the middle of the night or deranged junkies holding knives to my throat as hostage for a fix. His operation was perfectly invisible. A murmured phone call and the raw materials moved, a slip of paper passed and goods were distributed. I admired his efficiency the way you'd admire someone in the ship container business. He was even sort of aristocratic in a hillbilly kind of way. He'd give orders, occasionally check on his minions, but his heart was in the fox hunt which translated, for him, into shooting the heads off of wild turkeys while standing on the side of the freeway.

Lamborghinis and Italian suits don't go over real well in farm towns. If the Godfather had grown up hauling compost he too might have invested instead in high-quality red-and-black wool products when the money started flowing in. He might have spent his Sundays mushroom hunting and knocking around in a dented, primer-black twenty-year-old convertible Charger. For me, Paul's John Deere hat clutched to my head, bombing through the long flat roads in that roaring convertible with dead turkeys at my feet was a thrill the likes of which I had never known.

For his part, I think Paul was looking for a project. He was feeling a little stuck just dealing drugs, hanging out in hot tubs with prostitutes and remodeling his kitchen. I seemed like someone with a problem he could fix. You see, problem solving was his thing. He could solve a twelve-letter anagram in the amount of time it takes to roll a hundred dollar bill into a tube. He could also figure out how to get a man to commandeer a helicopter and fly undetected in broad daylight to make a drop of a two-hundred-pound bundle three states away. That was just his way. He got a charge out of a good brain tease. The main problem of mine that needed fixing, it turned out, was my youth. In Paul's view I was living a life without consequence. I was frivolous and unmoored. And he was appalled by the way I had been raised: My parents had let me stay out as long as I wanted at night, allowed me to drop out of high school for that peace march and encouraged me to move to Africa on my own. Most of all, he was completely taken aback by the fact that they had never instilled in me proper study habits.

He did have a point. After all, it was my failure to sit down and read a flimsy school brochure that had landed me in the Hawkeye state in the first place. Paul could fix that. Under his tutelage I would become focused and calm. I would no longer find myself unwittingly moving to top hog-producing areas. I could, in fact, possibly control my destiny. Paul, aside from all that cocaine, seemed like a good influence, and I figured I could use some guidance.

I moved most of my stuff to his house, an old two-bedroom farmhouse perpetually under construction located across town from campus. The house had two rooms upstairs: One was Paul's bedroom and the other, a small room with cans of dried paint for chairs, became my study. Every day when I came back from school he'd send me to my room, close the door, and instruct me not to come out until I finished all of my homework. Then, I could go to the bar, play with his guns, whatever. But that wasn't all. Paul made me dentist appointments and then paid the bills. He had me throw out my striped tube socks and bought me elegant dark gray ones. He switched my hair conditioner, which didn't control my frizz well enough, and worked on my penmanship; then he decided to do something about my choice of friends.

I didn't have many friends in Iowa, but the ones I had, I'd worked really hard to get. Jenny was my dorm roommate. whom I'd met about four days into the semester (because I'd misplaced my admissions letter and thought school started a week later). That day, carrying my bags through the dorm, I had noted every door I passed on the long hall was open, inviting in any passerby, and each room looked exactly the same. Then, at the very end, I reached my room. The door was closed, a Do Not Disturb sign on the doorknob. Ignoring it, I knocked. When no one answered, I opened the door and stepped inside a Goth palace, a coven of black and maroon velvet. Immense stone pillars, taller than I, were placed around the tiny room. The pink tile floor was covered with a plush black rug. I saw more Cure and Smiths records than I ever imagined existed. Two of the three beds were turned out with black sheets and fur duvets. Of the three desks, one was immaculately arranged with skull candles, another held rows of red lipstick and pale powders, and the last desk was bare except for a palm-sized voodoo doll, stuffed with pins, wearing a nametag—bearing my name. I plopped my stuff down and took a walk around the room, browsed through their mail, checked out their clothes and left. When I came back, there was a note on my desk: One does not wear shoes on the rug.

Jen and Jenny were best friends from Cedar Rapids. They had no other girl friends, but they were very well connected among the Cedar Rapids gay male community. They did not want another person in the room. They didn't need anyone else, particularly a messy, overly talkative roommate who shed curly hair all over the black rug. It took three months of talking incessantly, telling, I thought, hilarious story after hilarious story until Jen finally moved out and Jenny finally started laughing. It was exhausting but at last I had a friend who would go down with me to that basement bar where I met Paul and drink herself silly.

Paul decided that Jenny was too ridiculous for me. She was getting a reputation. She had been videotaped having sex with our bartender, and the final words on the tape, sure to get a laugh from the crowd watching were, "I promise I'll erase this tape if you let me do it in your butt . . . " Still, since her developing rep kept both her and her friends bathed in drinks on the house, I thought Jenny was a great companion.

But Paul thought I could do better, and decided I shouldn't talk to Jenny anymore. Instead, he thought I should spend more time with two of his friends. Steve was a professor of neuroscience. I don't remember what his girlfriend did because she didn't talk. When the four of us would get together, Paul and Steve would discuss events of the universe that I didn't understand even though, thanks to Paul's study routine, I was a 4.0 student majoring in astronomy. Still, I liked listening.

Occasionally I'd even learn something although I was always too terrified of embarrassing myself to ever actually speak. But it became hard, what with all that cocaine, to stay quiet for long.

Eventually I sought out Jenny again.

Jenny and I were discovered in a bar across town, famous as a hideout for couples having illicit affairs. Paul, being a drug dealer after all, had friends everywhere. Word got back, and that night Paul and I had a huge fight. I declared that I could do what I wanted, see whomever I chose. The more he treated me as if I were stupid, I told him, the stupider I was getting. I stormed out, slammed myself into my car and drove along the river, fuming, through dark, desolate farmland, past endless rows of tall, proud solitary stalks of corn and the dark shadows of lonely pigs housed individually in little huts. As I drove, I began to feel more sad than angry. If I gave up Paul, what would I do with my time? Go back to the dorm and try to get invited to a flavored-popcorn party with the girls? Paul still looked better to me than any of my other options. He took me places I wouldn't see without him, and introduced me to people I wouldn't otherwise meet. If only I could get a little more respect from him, our relationship might turn out okay. I'd go back, I decided, assert myself, demand some changes and start anew.

I got back to his house after midnight. He always kept his door unlocked, so I just walked in and went up the stairs to his bedroom. I opened the door and found Paul, lying on his stomach on the bed, staring at me. First I noticed the powder under his nose; then, I saw that he was pointing a shotgun directly at my chest. I couldn't move and, though I wanted to, I couldn't scream. Paul kept the gun pointed at me. He said I should never, ever, enter his house without announcing who I was. There were people who would kill him for his drugs, how could I not know that? I stood there, frozen in place. Paul slowly put the gun down, rolled over, took one last look at my face and said, "Go wash up."

How had it come to this? There I stood in a room filled with coke and ammo. My boyfriend, now oblivious to my presence, was manically flipping through the I Ching and wiping his nose. By comparison, my clothes matched, my shoes were shined, my new credit cards were safe in a new wallet, tucked away in my very first purse, and my teeth were absolutely tartar free. I stood there, all fixed up, for this?

I knew then that I had made a horrible miscalculation. I had mistaken what I didn't know for wisdom. Whatever "wisdom" Paul had didn't seem that desirable anymore. In just a few minutes, he shrunk in my eyes and any power he had had over me was gone.

I had already applied to another school, was leaving Iowa at the end of the semester. A repentant Paul hovered over me, trying to buy me new school clothes, but Jenny and I were consumed with a diligent and exhaustive quest to find her a new bar, one without a VCR, and in my spare time I was trying to figure out how to rig all those crazy Gothic pillars she had given me to the roof of my car. Finally on a bright spring day, in a flurry, with Jenny exploding a celebratory can of Budweiser over my car, I got out of town. It wasn't until I crossed the Mississippi River and eased off the bridge onto Wisconsin soil that I realized I had forgotten to say goodbye to Paul.

London Frog

M. Jane McKittrick

I arrived at LaGuardia Airport with an address scribbled on a scrap of paper and all my worldly possessions in four suitcases. Leaving behind the flat midwestern prairie, I was on my way to a pediatric nursing job in a big New York City hospital. Squeaky clean, straight off the farm and at the ripe old age of twenty-four, I was searching for adventure and eager to do my part to save the world, one child at a time.

A kind gentleman helped me drag my suitcases to the taxi stand. I slid onto the back seat of the cab and recited the address to the cabby. "Manhattan?" he asked. A momentary panic set in. At the time, I had no idea that New York City consisted of five boroughs, much less to which one I was headed. "Yeah, Manhattan," I answered, trying to appear composed. The cabby glanced back at me. "You wanna take the Midtown Tunnel or the Fifty-ninth Street Bridge?" *Great,* I thought. *He's asking me for directions?* "Either one," I said, hedging my bets. Thirty harrowing minutes later, I was safe inside my tiny efficiency apartment in the nurses' quarters on East Sixty-third Street.

"What? Are you crazy? You don't *evah* let a strangah handle your bags. You *nevah* get into a cab unless you know exactly where you're going! Do they even have traffic lights where you come from?"

That was Dorie, my next-door neighbor and self-appointed caretaker. Dorie was the classic New Yorker in every respect: the clothes, the nasal "get outta heah" accent and the unwavering attitude of self-assurance that comes from knowing that New York is the center of the universe.

Dorie, herself, was an educational institution. Not just a professor in the fine art of New York chutzpah, she was also the dean of sexuality. Dorie wasn't sexy in the classic sense—not by a long shot. She had long, nondescript brown hair and tweezed eyebrows, wore lots of makeup and was almost but not quite plump. Dorie was the only person I'd seen, aside from TV or movie characters, who had to lie down flat on her back to zip her jeans. But she was a bona fide sex magnet for men. With a perfected toss of the ponytail, a coy tilt of the head, a flippant hand gesture and a magnificent hip-swiveling gait, she didn't just command attention from men, she demanded it. She was carnal cocaine, a sexual narcotic.

Compared to Dorie, I was a nun. I had long since resigned myself to the fact that I was never going to be stunning, exquisite, ravishing or alluring. At five foot two, with a round face, turned up nose, curly red hair and freckles, I was fatally cute in a Shirley Temple or Doris Day kind of way. I told myself it could be worse. Cute isn't all that bad—if you like getting your cheeks pinched by old ladies. But cute just doesn't cut it if you want to attract men: real men who take you in their arms and call you "darling" and ravish you and make you feel like a sex goddess. Dorie was a sex goddess. I was a pixie.

"Geez, Jane, you're a real barrel of laughs. All you evah do is work and come home to your crummy little apartment. Why don't you go out with me tonight?" Dorie was blowing on the wet fingernails of one hand while reaching for a potato chip with the other.

"Like where?" I asked. "You know I hate pickup bars."

"Then let's just go out to dinner," she suggested. "No pickup bars, I promise."

Our first stop was the Oak Room at the Plaza. "I thought you said no bars," I complained. "I said no pickup bars," she reminded me. "Look around, already. Does this look like a pickup joint?" She was right. The place was regal, filled with lawyers making high-priced deals and dark, massive oil paintings, and it generally reeked of old money and tradition. I ordered a scotch on the rocks, not because I particularly liked scotch; I couldn't think of anything else sophisticated enough on short notice.

I was sitting at the bar with Dorie, trying to look like I belonged there, when a balding, middle-aged man in an expensive suit staggered up to us. "You girlsh got a room?" He reeked of alcohol and could barely stand.

"Beat it, mistah," Dorie hissed, but he was a man on a mission.

"I jusht wanted to know if you girlsh got a room."

Dorie turned on him, pointed a lacquered nail in his face and snarled, "I said get outta heah! Leave us alone!" With that, the drunk stumbled away.

"Nice way to treat an old drunk guy, Dorie," I remarked. "Did you have to be so mean?" She looked at me like I was nuts.

"You've really got a lot to learn, kid. He thought we were hookahs." I was in utter disbelief.

"You mean us? *Me?*"

Dorie shot me a look of sheer exasperation. "Yeah, you."

Eventually we found a French bistro, a romantic little place crammed with tables for two decked in white linens, sprigs of freesia and candles. Still laughing about the drunk at the Oak Room, we ordered wine and settled in for a nice, quiet evening. Then the sideshow began.

At the table just behind us sat a man and woman straight out of a circus trailer. The man started pulling long strands of brightly colored scarves out of his sleeves. Bouquets of feathery flowers appeared out of thin air, then a pack of oversized playing cards, more corny tricks. His partner filled the room with high-pitched laugher, and in accordance with strict New York protocol for situations like this, Dorie and I joined with the rest of the patrons in pretending not to notice.

Our façade of cool detachment was suddenly breached by a voice from the table to our right. "Would you mind awfully if we borrowed your salt? Ours seems to have gone missing."

A savvy New Yorker might have smelled a rat with the old missing-saltshaker gambit, but not yours truly. I was instantly taken in by the two well-dressed British gentlemen seated next to us—not by their looks, but by their Oxford-educated, Masterpiece Theatre accents. The saltshaker inevitably led to further conversation: How about that chap doing the conjuring tricks? Where are you ladies from? They were interesting, worldly corporate attorneys for an international oil company. Perfect gentlemen. Surely there was no harm in taking them up on their offer of a drink after dinner.

The four of us walked to a nearby bar and before I realized what was happening, we were paired off, Dorie with one and I with the other. I ordered a glass of wine; he ordered a shandy— half lemonade, half beer. *Perfectly harmless,* I told myself. Nobody who wasn't upright would order a drink like that.

His name was Colin, a tall, well-built man in his early thirties. He was more charming than handsome, charming enough to compensate for a drooping right eyelid. *In another time he'd be wearing a monocle,* I thought. At least it seemed like a truly British aristocratic flaw, and it was his Britishness that attracted me most.

He said he was in New York for the first time and he wondered what sights he should see. Could I recommend any?

Flattered by his attention, his assumption that I was a seasoned New Yorker, and under the influence of more alcohol than I was used to, I babbled on about the Statue of Liberty, Rockefeller Center, Radio City Music Hall, the Empire State Building. "I'm flying back to London in the morning, but I plan to come back in the near future. Perhaps you'd be kind enough to take me sightseeing next time I'm in the city?" *Sure, why not?* I thought. After all, he was just a nice, clean cut, educated professional guy who needed someone to show him the sights. What could be the harm of that? I was sure he was safe. I gave him my phone number.

Dorie and I took the subway home. "Colin asked me if I would take him sightseeing next time he's in New York," I announced with breathless excitement.

"You gave him your phone number?!" she screamed. "You really are a country bumpkin, aren't you? He isn't going to call. He was just chatting you up. The other old geezah is married with three kids, and Colin probably is too. Forget about it."

So I did. Or at least I tried to put it out of my mind as I went about my work in the pediatric wards. I worked extra shifts, stayed late, dragged my exhausted body home day after day, no love life in sight. Two months later the phone rang.

"Dorie! He called! Colin actually called! I'm meeting him for lunch tomorrow!" I wanted Dorie to be excited for me.

"Well," she said, evaluating the situation, "at least you're meeting him at the University Club. It's a male chauvinist fortress. No women allowed. At least he won't be able to drag you into his room."

"Thanks for your support," I muttered. But even Dorie's jaundiced opinion couldn't dampen my spirits. What did she know about Colin, anyway? She was too busy enticing guys into her web to have any sense of real romance.

It took some doing to muster up enough courage to keep my date with Colin. Despite my nervousness and second thoughts, I steeled myself and marched bravely into the University Club, where an attendant in a red blazer instantly accosted me. "Women are allowed only in the ladies' waiting room," he informed me in the nastiest tone possible. He was thrusting his arm in the direction of the parlor where I would be sequestered until further notice, when Colin came to my rescue. "It's all right, she's with me." With that, he whisked me to the elevator and up to the formal dining room, where women were rarely and begrudgingly allowed to dine.

It was exactly as I pictured it. Old men in red leather wing chairs, smoking cigars, sipping port, reading the *Wall Street Journal,* and none too happy to have me in their privileged domain. White-jacketed waiters, men who would never in a million years be allowed on the premises except as servants, bowed and scraped. The old men grunted. The food was mediocre, and the conversation was awkward. I couldn't get out of there fast enough.

After lunch we took in a Broadway matinee of *Guys and Dolls.* Colin couldn't have seen much of it; for two hours he stared longingly at my profile. I wasn't sure if it was creepy or sweet. When the play was over, we walked for what seemed like hours in the cold October air through Chinatown, Little Italy and Greenwich Village. He was totally smitten with me, I could tell, and though I was feeling cautious, I was warming up to him slowly but surely.

It was getting late, but neither of us was ready to part. We stopped at a coffee house on Spring Street for cappuccino and sat at a table by the window, watching people go by and chatting about all sorts of things. When the conversation turned to the high cost of living in England, I saw my big chance. Trying my utmost to be nonchalant, or at least not too pathetically obvious, I said, "Well, you're lucky you don't have children to put through college. It costs a fortune these days." He became very quiet. An anguished look came over his face and tears welled up in his eyes. "The truth is," he said, "I do have children. Two young daughters."

I was debating whether or not to take a swing at him before I got up to leave, when I realized he was actually crying. Colin continued, haltingly, choking back his tears, "My wife was killed in a car crash two years ago. My daughters and I are all alone." He filled in some of the details about a wet road, a drunk driver, but I didn't hear much of it. I was too busy kicking myself for having doubted him. My heart ached for him. As he cried, I held his hand across the table. I was falling for him in a big way.

The cab ride to my apartment was quiet and intimate. Colin walked me to the door, gazed at me with tears in his eyes and said, "You're marvelous, you're wonderful. I don't know when I've enjoyed the company of a woman so much, but I'm afraid I can never see you again. I can't explain it adequately. I just can't see you again." He kissed me on the cheek, got back in the waiting cab, and that was that.

I tried, unsuccessfully, to sneak past Dorie's apartment unseen. She really missed her calling; the CIA could have used an interrogator like her. "So let me get this straight," she began. "First he's mad about you, then he can't see you again." Too exhausted to argue, I simply nodded. "Yeah, that's it. I don't know what to think. Maybe he's still too upset about his wife dying or something." She shot me that look of hers again. "Yeah. Or something."

Early the next morning the phone awakened me. It was Colin. "I can't believe what a fool I am. I can't believe I ever thought it would be possible not to see you again. You're the most incredible woman I've ever met. Please, please say you'll have dinner with me tonight." And so I did.

That was the beginning of a whirlwind romance straight out of a Danielle Steele novel. Colin jetted around the world on the Concorde, and once a month his business brought him to New York for a few days. When he was in New York, I lived like a queen: the Metropolitan Opera, symphony concerts, museums, Broadway plays, taxi cabs, limousines, the finest French restaurants (he ordered in fluent French, of course). And when he wasn't in New York, he called faithfully once a week from London, wrote love letters almost daily and sent me jewelry, perfume, flowers and chocolates. It was all too good to be true, and yet it was true. For the first time in my life I felt truly adored.

One evening in February, after the theater and a cozy late dinner at my apartment, Colin turned from my embrace and began to cry. I tried everything I knew to get him to talk to me. He was inconsolable; I was becoming alarmed. Finally he regained his composure and began his confession. "I don't know how to tell you. I'm so afraid of losing you. The truth is that my wife isn't dead. Ever since the accident she's been in a coma, a vegetative state. The doctors give her no chance of ever recovering. She may languish that way for years . . ."

We talked for hours, late into the night. I promised I would not desert him. I begged him to realize that he was entitled to have a life, that living without joy and pleasure wouldn't help his wife or his children. Ultimately I convinced him—and myself—that our relationship wasn't necessarily a betrayal of his marriage. After hours of talking and rationalizing, Colin seemed relieved and comforted. I knew things would never be the same.

Dorie was no help. "So you're telling me that first she's dead and now she's been upgraded to comatose. Is that what you're telling me? Wait, let me call the *Journal of the American Medical Association*. This is some kind of miracle." Her cynicism was getting on my nerves.

"Your compassion is really overwhelming, Dorie," I snapped, as I turned to leave her apartment.

"Yeah?" she yelled after me. "Well, what you don't know about men I could write a book about!"

The calls, the love letters, the trips to New York, the flowers and theater continued for a few more months. But without the twinkle, without the fairy dust. Still, I held out hope that things would return to the way they were in the beginning, when everything was fresh and wild and breathtaking.

For more than six months romance had triumphed over reason, but even I was savvy enough to realize that it was all going to end sooner or later. In May I received three numbered letters from Colin. A series. Read this one first, this one second and so on. In an instant Colin had sunk from the romantic master of fluent French and the Queen's English to a letter-writing ploy not even worthy of a junior-high skirt chaser. I knew without opening them what the letters were all about.

The first letter began, *My dearest Love, I apologise that my tears are staining this letter* (in case I hadn't noticed the water stains). There followed tons of lovelorn drivel, and finally the upshot: His wife, alive and well, had found in his briefcase some letters he had written to me. He explained that he hadn't ever meant to be deceptive. It seems that his wife was such an unresponsive shrew that in his heart it really was as if she were dead. Or comatose. Or whatever.

The second letter was a little more upbeat. He was sure I'd be "glad to know" that after his wife calmed down about the letter and the affair, they had begun putting their marriage back together and that things between them were better than they had ever been. I was, of course, thrilled to know that.

The third letter detailed a plan whereby he would get his company to transfer him to the United States for two years and I would continue to see him, even though his wife and children would probably come with him. Brilliant idea! And then, in an act of impeccable timing, just as I finished reading the third letter, a deliveryman appeared with two dozen long-stemmed yellow roses with a card that read: *Je reviens. Love, Colin.*

Naturally, Dorie appeared on the heels of the delivery guy. I handed her the letters, and she read them without uttering a word. Not a single "I told you so," not a single "tsk, tsk." She disappeared back into her apartment and returned a moment later with a sheet of stationery, an envelope and a small bottle of contact lens solution.

Dear Colin, she wrote. *I am so sorry to have to inform you that Jane was involved in a tragic traffic accident two days ago. She languished in a coma until this afternoon, when she finally succumbed. Her husband is arriving from Denver tomorrow morning to collect her remains. I know she admired you for your caring and honesty. We will all miss her.*

She sprinkled a few drops of the contact lens solution on the page, just enough to smear the ink a little, and enclosed two yellow rose petals.

The Tao of Pizza and Sex

R. Gay

Scott Fitzer and I should never have been friends. He's a white boy Republican who still hangs out with his frat buddies even though he's been out of school for years. He plays harder than he works and prides himself on being blissfully ignorant. I, on the other hand, am neither white nor male nor Republican. Had we not met in a required sociology course during college, where we were forced to sit next to each other, we wouldn't have given each other the time of day. But despite our differences, Scott is indeed a charming guy and I've managed to learn a thing or two from him. He once told me that sex was like pizza. At first, I could not quite wrap my mind around the analogy. He sat me down, and explained to me in very simple terms that he had eaten pizza he wouldn't choose to eat again for a variety of reasons (too much sauce, too little cheese, anchovies, raw onions), and he had eaten pizza that he would love to have every day. But he had never regretted a single slice of pizza that had passed his lips, and his sexual liaisons were much the same. In his mind, there was no such thing as either bad sex or bad pizza. I found his logic absurd. While up until that point, I had never been party to bad sex, I had certainly eaten my share of bad pizza. In my mind, if it was possible for a pizza to taste like stale cat fur, it was certainly possible for two (or more) people to have an unfortunate sexual encounter. When Scott asked me how I could believe in the existence of something I had never experienced, I casually mentioned the small detail of his belief in God, and the conversation digressed from there.

Then I met a woman, whom I'll refer to as Cynthia, online, which in and of itself should have triggered a warning light on my mental dashboard. Cyberdating is always a tricky affair, what with the canyon between expectation and reality. Cynthia and I had exchanged pictures and she was cute enough, for a white girl, though in all her pictures, her cheeks were inexplicably rosy as if she were plagued by eternal cheer. It was her personality that really turned me on, however trite it may be to admit that. Cynthia had a charming naiveté about her that made me want to protect her and corrupt her at the same time. In our phone conversations, she made me laugh with her timid attempts at sexual innuendo, and she made my heart ache when, lowering her voice to just above a whisper, she would tell me that she was falling for me, scared, crazy even to think about love but willing to take the chance. After four months of flirtation and fantasy, we decided that meeting was imperative—we were ready to take our relationship to the next level. I was tired of fondling my computer monitor, and we could more wisely invest the phone bill money in airplane tickets. Cynthia lived in one of those frightening middle states so we decided that she would come to me, so to speak. She would only be in Phoenix, where I lived at the time, for three days, so the D.P. (Drama/Disaster Potential) hovered at an acceptable level. At the time, I was doing phone sex for work, so to be fair, I must confess that I was a little burned out on sex. Eight hours a night of telling Big Daddy how sweet the lovin' was made it rather difficult to turn around and tell my sweet mama that I was burnin', burnin' and rarin' to go. Nonetheless, every time I thought about seeing Cynthia in the airport or crawling into bed next to her warm body or tracing her contours with my lips, I felt a sharp, almost painful twinge between my thighs that I was certain only she could satisfy.

Fast forward to the Big Day. I was working the graveyard shift. Cynthia's plane arrived at 10 A.M., so I got off work without getting off at work, slept not at all and dragged my tired, cranky ass to the airport after running home to check my email. There was a message from her telling me how excited she was, what a wonderful weekend we were going to have, how we were going to christen every room with our blossoming love. I was nervous, and for the first time in my adult life, my palms began sweating. As I sat at the gate, waiting for her plane to arrive, I crossed and uncrossed my legs, wiping my hands against my jeans until there were damp smudges just above my knees. My tension was joined by a slight sense of nausea that only increased when Cynthia deplaned and I took note of the cute enough, rosy-cheeked white girl with exceptionally greasy hair. We hugged, she kissed my cheek and gave me what I perceived to be a meaningful look.

I sighed, which turned into a long yawn. Apologizing, I

rubbed my eyes and, holding her hands, stepped back. "Let me have a look at you," I murmured. She wore faded jeans and a clingy T-shirt that exposed an inch of creamy white skin just below her navel. In that moment, I seriously considered sneaking her into the nearby restroom to peel off her clothes so that someday we'd have an interesting story to tell our friends about the first time we met. Grinning, I squeezed Cynthia's hands a little harder and slowly twirled her around. I sucked on my teeth and inhaled sharply. The hair aside, Cynthia had a perfect ass, the kind a woman spends her whole life thanking her parents for, the kind I wanted to thank her parents for, round and soft and firm all at the same time. As we began walking toward the baggage claim, I lagged a few steps behind her, with an absurd grin on my face. All of a sudden, I felt rejuvenated. I couldn't wait to get home. I was certain that I had the most desirable woman on the planet, hanging on my arm. I had the world, in that brief moment, in the palm of my hand. And soon, I hoped, I would have the most delectable bits of Cynthia in that very same place.

In the car on the way home, she giggled and played with my neck and made suggestive comments that brought back that sharp twinge between my thighs. I lightly drew my fingers along her chin and neck to her collarbone, marveling at how soft her skin was. At the same time, I obsessed over my uncomfortable fascination with the hair, dear God, the hair—thick, shiny tufts of black hair pointed at awkward angles. "My dormmates and I were having a contest to see how long we could go without washing our hair," she offered by way of explanation. I arched an eyebrow and made an addendum to my mental notebook about the strange hygiene habits of white girls. Gripping the steering wheel so hard my knuckles turned an interesting shade of gray, I remembered her voice, when it lowered to just above a whisper, and smiled.

By the time we reached my apartment, I had passed fatigue and reached the kind of exhaustion where I didn't have the energy to focus on much of anything beyond my need for uninterrupted sleep. Cynthia offered to give me a shoulder rub so I fell face down onto my futon, thankful for the reprieve from conversation, but of course, as lesbians often do, she felt the need to process the initial moments of our visit. She babbled about how nervous she was on the plane, how our attraction had indeed carried into reality, how she was feeling really positive about our impending journey together. I grunted occasionally, because while I agreed for the most part, I was at once too tired to share in the process and too polite to ask her to wash her hair. Suddenly, I felt something cool and slithery against the back of my neck. I tried my best to swat it away, certain that some roach or gecko had stealthily crept past the poisoned traps and into my bedroom. Both are very real possibilities when living in the desert.

Through the haze of fatigue, I realized that the slithery thing was Cynthia's tongue and before I knew it, she had flipped me onto my back and yanked my shirt over my head. "I haven't been properly laid in over a year," she whispered, pressing her bulk against me. Neither had I, but I wasn't going to admit it. I bit my lower lip and winced, trying tactfully to roll her to the side. She thought I was being frisky and pinned my arms over my head. I quickly assessed the situation and realized that the easiest way to extract myself from her grip and get some sleep was to do the dirty deed as quickly as possible. I smiled again, moaned softly and wrapped my legs around her waist. I remembered that first glimpse of her bare waist and began lazily splaying my fingers under her shirt, against the small of her back. It felt good, after all this time, to have her this close.

I should have seen the signs. The hair was a clear indicator, but again, I was tired. My eyelids were heavy. My mind was slow. This is what I tell myself now, to soothe myself, to ease the trauma. Cynthia cooed, stood up and quickly undressed. Again, to be fair, she had that killer body. Round, soft breasts that felt so smooth and heavy in my hands that I was willing to forgive the hair. Swollen pink nipples. Thick thighs and casually sculpted calves. Her stunning ass, so subtly curved, bringing forth images of all things ripe and willing to be plucked. But none of that was enough to distract from a very distinct body odor. She had the nerve to act shy for a moment. "I didn't have time to shower this morning, do you mind?" I swallowed, hard, and shook my head. "I love a woman's natural scent," I told her, which was, in part, true. But in my mind, there was a fine line between delighting in natural odors and suffocating in unnatural rank. She lay on my futon, and I knelt between her legs, brushing my lips along her arms, holding my breath as I reached her shoulders, kissing and licking her neck, trying to arouse myself by imagining how wonderful she would look freshly scrubbed. "I love pussy. I can do this," I kept reminding myself. "What was that?" she asked. "I've been waiting so long to do this."

It is odd what you remember about sexual encounters. I remember that we did not kiss, and that not kissing was one of the more disappointing elements of the entirely disappointing Cynthia ordeal. The fact is that a kiss is intimate, perhaps even more intimate than making love. Most of my friends claim that they are more eager to have sex with someone than to engage in a kiss. Sex can be detached, bodies barely touching, but a kiss done properly is face to face, skin to skin, lips and tongues and teeth in a tangle. And perhaps this is why the art of the kiss is dying. We are afraid of the self-exposure that occurs when lips brush together. I wanted to kiss Cynthia because you can learn a lot from a woman by how she kisses, but at the same time, I was terrified with what I might find between her lips. I could not deny the possibility that she was also in a contest with someone as to who could amass the most plaque.

So there I was, trying to be sensual, focusing a great deal of attention on her breasts, which had become a scent-free oasis. I suckled and nipped and twisted her nipples with my lips and tongue and fingers until she was quivering and on the verge of tears. I worshipped her breasts for what they weren't. "You redefine foreplay," she gasped, and I choked back a laugh, because indeed, a part of me could see the humor in the situation. "You inspire me," I told her, and promised myself to say twelve Hail Marys when I got the chance. I was a good

Catholic girl, after all. Her fingers snaked through my hair, urging my head lower, and I knew that sooner or later, I would have to go down. *I'm strong,* I told myself. *I can handle this.* Of course, hours earlier, I had dealt with a customer who called himself Pee Wee and spent half an hour, $120 and a good deal of my patience telling me about all his truly unique sexual peccadilloes. In Cynthia's defense, my tolerance was at an all-time low, so I redoubled my efforts.

I dragged my lips across her torso, dipping my tongue inside her navel, before tracing her waist with my fingertips. I kissed her inner thighs and under her knees and the soft inner spots of her ankles and congratulated myself on the thorough job I was doing, kissing everything but the clit. Then Cynthia said she couldn't take it anymore. There was an edge to her voice—an urgency that let me know, in no uncertain terms, that it was *go* time. I summoned my courage and I'll be damned if I didn't think about pizza. I crawled up her thighs and tried to distract her with my fingers, circling her clit with my thumb, letting my fingers safely slip inside her. "I want you to taste me," Cynthia groaned, and suddenly I knew that there was no delicate way to avoid the unavoidable. I regretted so many things in that moment—not reading "Miss Manners," cruising along the

109

Information Superhighway, not entering a convent. It was a moment of startling clarity—when good lesbians smell bad. I lowered my lips to hers and began licking as quickly as possible. I valiantly tried to ignore the taste and the smell and the fact that I was turning blue. I was racked with guilt because I'm always glorifying pussy and chastising my male friends who complain about the not-so-fresh factor, which to that point, I had vehemently denied the existence of. And I thought that perhaps I was indeed too tired to give Cynthia the chance she deserved, that after a nice long nap, I would remember our all-night phone conversations and the sweet care packages she sent now and then and the very distinct possibility that I loved her—all the reasons that this visit had come to pass. But as her sour taste rolled down the back of my throat and stayed there, interminably, I was forced to accept that some things are unforgivable.

The remaining details don't matter, but there are a few facts of note in the aftermath. Cynthia promptly fell asleep after locking my neck between her thighs in the throes of an orgasm. I won't even get into how long it took for her to reach those throes, but I will say that three different albums cycled through my CD player. I never did get sleep that afternoon because I was at the chiropractor, receiving a much-needed adjustment. Cynthia did not shower for the remainder of the visit but insisted we have sex at every turn. I never got laid because her first snore promptly arrived on the heels of her last orgasmic shudder. Shortly after her plane arrived back in the middle states, Cynthia called me. I was lying in my bed, alone, for the first time in days and quite happy about it. She began gushing about what a wonderful time she'd had with me, how she couldn't wait until our next visit, and I could literally hear my self-control snapping, with a sharp ping. In no uncertain terms, I told her that while she had a lovely personality, unless she drastically altered her hygiene regimen, there would be no more visits. Cynthia was so offended that she hung up on me, and I fell fast asleep, luxuriating in my freedom. I never heard from her again.

When I had sufficiently recovered from the ordeal, I invited Scott to my place. He sat on my couch, a sweaty beer resting between his denim-clad thighs, a smug expression on his face as he waited for me to brief him on my short-lived affair. Instead, I presented him with a cream cheese, tomato, liver and tongue pizza, which I enjoyed because my taste buds were mostly dead. As for Scott, he now believes in bad sex.

Demon Lover

Elizabeth Mathews

I had a feeling the first time I saw him. That feeling was repulsion. I was sitting outside at my friend's place when he strolled out of the house with his weird rolling walk, bobbing his head from side to side to make his long curls fly around. He stopped in front of me, and while I was taking in his strange combination of biker jacket and dress pants, he flashed me a wolfish grin and said, "So, this must be Melissa." I snapped that no, my name is Elizabeth, and went inside, regretting that I hadn't told him my name was Zelda Pinwheel.

Max had wormed his way into my circle of friends a few weeks before, though none would admit to liking him. In general we were a pretty accepting crowd, geeky and shy but welcoming. Yet for some reason Max rubbed us all the wrong way. Maybe it was his suspiciously good looks, or the fact that he was swimming in friends of the non-outcast variety. We also figured out pretty quickly that he reeked of sleaze, addressing all women as "Sweets" or "Darlin' " and consorting with multiple bed buddies. I, being easily appalled, was appalled by Max from the start.

Despite all this, he stuck around and quickly developed an affinity for me, although I was at best passive and at worst cruel to him. He had a habit of cornering me and saying vague, lovesick things that flattered and intrigued me but also forced me to mock him. A couple of weeks after we first met, I went to a friend's Halloween party. I had thrown together a costume at the last minute, consisting of a few layers of raggedy dresses decorated with silver spray paint, which I told people made me "Luna, you know, like the moon." The party swarmed with people I didn't know, so I was self-consciously waiting it out in a corner when Max made his entrance. He turned his head my way several times while working the room, and then ambled over. Pretending not to see me, he sank into the chair next to mine with a sigh. "What's wrong?" I asked, taking the bait.

"I . . . I can't tell you."

"Why are you wearing sunglasses in a dark room? Is that your costume?"

"No. I need the shades because you're so . . . bright."

"Yeah. I'm the moon."

"No. No. I mean (hair toss), you glow. Your aura is blinding me."

"Max?"

"Yes?"

"Just how much crack have you been smoking?"

Max became the only thing marring my otherwise idyllic social set. In my suburban hometown I was an oddity: too poorly dressed and badly dyed to blend in with the well-groomed teen offspring of wealthy Bellevue couples. Too shy and eager to please to cultivate the fuck-you attitude of the other freaks I knew, I sought most of my social interaction through my computer. It was there that I met the people who would become my group for the next several years. The first time I saw them in person, I was shocked by their faded black metal T-shirts and their butt-rock hair, and creeped out by their casual references to New Agey phenomena. It took some adjusting, but once I got past all that I was delighted. Finally, I had found people I could be comfortable with.

I would bus the two hours out of Bellevue into the nastiest neighborhood in south Seattle to sit in a smoke-filled room, listen to computerized music, talk about crystals and channeling, and recite my latest attempts at poetry. My mostly male friends adored me, as I was one of the only girls willing to embrace their computers-and-fantasy world. Ricky was my boyfriend at the time. He liked to be called Tinkerbell because he believed he had the soul of a fairy. He was a sweet guy, but a huge flirt.

To cement our group friendship, we role-played, Dungeons and Dragons–style, once a week. Every Saturday, we got together and pretended to be our characters, usually elves or gnomes with names like Shalandra and Tor, and we embarked on imaginary journeys through caves of bones or villages with taverns operated by surly centaurs. We spoke in what we imagined to be medieval English and battled dragons and ogres by rolling dice. We were totally unaware of how dorky this made us.

Max insisted on joining us, and I soon found that he was more melodramatic than all of us put together. One day, while role-playing, a monster killed his character. Max argued with the gamemaster that he should be brought back to life. As the rest of us perched nervously around the table, sensing a scene, the gamemaster tried to pacify him. "Okay, Max, roll two twenty-sided dice, and if you get higher than a fifteen, Zorbie has a chance of being resurrected." With the utmost solemnity, Max stood, picked up the dice and kissed them. He closed his eyes, shook the dice and rolled them gently onto the table. A two and a three. Around the table, we chorused, "Aw, too bad, man." But Max didn't stop there.

"I'm summoning all of my energy, and with my dying breath I'm saying a prayer to the demon lord Mygara, asking that he save me."

"Max, you can't. You're dead. Your head was liquefied, dude."

"Then I'm rising from the underworld to tell the other characters how to revive me."

"Sorry, Max." At this point Max's eyes began to flash, and his nostrils flared. He banged his fist on the table.

"It's not fair! Zorbie was my best character ever!" His face swelled red, and with horror I realized he was going to cry.

"Umm, Max? Do you want to take a break, go outside or something?" He shook his head violently. After sending a death-beam glare around the room, he threw himself back in his chair, pulled two cigarettes from his pack, lit them both and puffed away in silence. Tears streamed down his face.

Although I had made a sport of mocking Max, we slowly became friends. He endured all my teasing and stuck around to keep me company when Ricky was off chasing young teens. He let me whine about my relationship without ever suggesting that I was an idiot to put up with it, and I appreciated that. Plus, with all his high drama, he could be pretty entertaining. He acted out heroic street fights for me and detailed his encounters with a woman who had led him to become a creature who drained energy from others in order to live. "Like a vampire?" I asked.

"No, I wasn't a vampire. And besides, I can control it better now."

"Is that why you wear so much black? Because you're a vampire?"

"No!"

I don't recall ever making an effort to see him. Somehow he would just appear. At first he was just a welcome distraction from whatever angst I was embroiled in, but he came to be a comforting presence. I looked forward to seeing him and stepping into his world.

Ricky finally broke up with me in the spring because, as he told me, he needed to come to terms with his dark side. As it turned out, all he needed to do was sleep with a bunch of girls.

Anyway, such was my confidence in Max's extrasensory perception that I was surprised the news didn't reach him for three days. Of course, Max was on the phone as soon as he heard, consoling me, cursing that unfeeling bastard, letting me sob to him for hours.

He invited me to the Seattle Center that weekend, ostensibly to cheer me up, but I could tell he had other things on his mind. We walked in circles around the fountain while I talked about my broken heart. He was unusually quiet, making sympathetic faces but obviously distracted. When we came to a gnarled tree draped with belated Christmas lights, he suggested we sit. I flopped down on the patchy grass, and he leaned against the tree, crossing his arms and looking at his boots. "Elizabeth, I have something to tell you." I was suddenly overcome with excitement and dread.

"What is it?"

"No . . . I can't tell you."

"Yes, you can."

"I really can't. It's wrong."

"Tell me."

"No."

"Tell me."

"No." He looked tortured, and I decided to let the subject drop. A minute later he burst out with: "I can't hide it any longer! Elizabeth, I love you. I've loved you since I first saw you. I know it's unforgivable, but I can't help myself. You're beautiful and wise, and you have the most shining soul I've ever seen." He watched hopefully for my reaction.

"Oh. Umm, wow. Shit. That's . . . damn."

"You don't have to say anything now. I just had to tell you." He helped me to my feet, and we started walking downtown to my bus. I felt strangely giddy, and after a few blocks he slipped his hand into mine. With that, I allowed myself to become the queen of his strange kingdom.

Things between us were a bit clunky from the beginning. Because he lived in a hotel with his mom and I lived far away from his preferred territory, we would meet in the parks in his neighborhood to make out. Parks where dog owners did not routinely clean up after their dogs. Soon, I associated the act of kissing him with the smell of dog shit. Without noticing it, I made a habit of resting my hands on his chest when he kissed me, so I could push him away when I got disgusted by his rotting teeth or the way he shoved his tongue down my throat. But I overlooked this and many other things. Once we started dating, I became fiercely protective of him, which was not completely unnecessary since most of my friends threatened to break Max's legs if he hurt my feelings. I became adept at making excuses for him, explaining why he had dropped out of high school, why he had never had a job, why he acted so weird, why he moved out of his mother's hotel room to stay on my friends' couch.

One night he staggered into my friends' apartment with a wild look on his face. He pulled me into one of the bedrooms and, shaking, told me what had happened. He had gone out to get cigarettes and had encountered his archnemesis, a girl named Spiral. "I could've handled it if it had been just her, but she was with these two huge guys." He pantomimed someone with the proportions of the Incredible Hulk. "They had me surrounded!" He acted out looking from left to right and backing away. He narrowed his eyes. He growled. "Then all three of them came at me at once. I dodged and kicked one in the back, but they closed in on me." He crouched low and started swinging his arms around, blocking imaginary punches and kicks, jabbing at the air, baring his teeth. "I fought them until they ran away, but my leg got fucked up pretty bad, and Spiral got me with her claws." He tugged at the back of his shirt to reveal bright scratches. I cooed sympathetically, but couldn't help eyeing his very long nails with suspicion.

"Go on," I said warily.

"Now, I want you to listen carefully. I buried a box of my things at Seahurst Beach—some very important papers and ritual stones and my lucky casting amulet. If Spiral and her thugs get hold of me, I need you to go there and dig it up to keep it safe from my enemies." I felt a chill run through me.

"Where did you bury it?"

"On one of the trails in the woods by the beach. First, find the trail with two trees growing together. Walk up the trail twenty paces. You'll see a bush with red berries. Under the bush is a rock with my symbol on it, you know, the cross with four stars around it. That's where you'll dig." I committed this information to memory, and for the next week I lived in terror that I would have to use it. But after a few days he grew bored with having Spiral as an archnemesis and was on the prowl for a new adventure.

Meanwhile our relationship was also getting dull. Perhaps to make himself look better, Max became intent on putting down my ex-boyfriend. Ricky became our favorite topic of conversation once we ran out of other things to talk about, which happened quickly. Max salivated every time he acquired a bit of gossip to deliver to me: Ricky lost his job at the market and has to beg his friends for handouts; Ricky is dating a fifteen-year-old; Ricky peed his pants in public.

One day Max asked to borrow the crystal that Ricky had given me for my birthday: a huge chunk of rock that he insisted I keep sheathed in leather to protect it. I handed it over readily enough. "What do you want it for?" I asked Max as an afterthought.

"This crystal holds the soul of a Minotaur, trapped for centuries. I think that if I can release it, it will be that bastard Ricky's downfall."

"Okay," I said, thinking there could be no harm in humoring him, and I quickly forgot about it. A few nights later I got a call from Max, breathless with glee.

"I did it!" he crowed.

"Did what?"

"I smashed the crystal to dust."

"What? Why did you do that?"

"I told you—the Minotaur. But that's not the best part. Ricky was over here role-playing, and I walked up to him—he was sitting on the floor making a character—and I stood over him and poured the crystal dust in his lap. Then I told him what it was, and I said, 'Next time, it'll be you.' You should have seen it! He went white, and then he jumped up and just ran out the door. Someone went after him, but he just took off."

I started to feel queasy. I suddenly remembered what Ricky had said when he gave me the crystal, that it was one of the only things he had to remember his recently departed grandmother by. It dawned on me that our game had gone too far. I no longer felt like the tragic heroine. I felt like shit. "You have to go find him and make sure he's okay," I said.

"Wait, didn't you hear what I just said? He's vanquished! We won! After this, he's gonna think twice before messing with us."

"Listen, I can't look for him myself; I'm miles away and the buses quit running at ten. If you don't find him before he does something stupid . . . this is our fault, Max."

He sighed loudly. "Fine. I'll look for him. I'll make nice. I'll get little Ricky home safe and sound, but only to make you happy. I don't care if that fucker offs himself." The words were like a steel-toed boot stomping on my foot. I hung up the phone and wondered how I had gotten mixed up with this person.

Hours passed as I waited to hear from Max. The phone

finally rang around one o'clock. "Hello? Elizabeth?" a small voice asked.

"Max? What happened? Where have you been?"

"I'm in jail." He explained that when he was out looking for Ricky, the police stopped him. He looked like one of the suspects in a convenience-store robbery. They figured out he was the wrong guy, but while they were running him through their computer, they discovered he had a three-year-old outstanding warrant for shoplifting. "Be brave," he said. "Wait for me. And remember—I don't blame you for this."

I spent the next few days putting the pieces of my life back together. It turned out Ricky had sulked in a park for a few hours and gone home. I swallowed my ex-girlfriend bitterness and made up with him. I also suffered through endless conversations with Max from his jail cell. He had arranged for a friend's mother to pay his bail, adding five hundred dollars to the debts he had been racking up since I met him. He told me he feared he would return a hardened man.

The day he was released I spent my two-hour bus ride going over everything in my head. For the first time, I was able to add things up: my lack of attraction to him, his irresponsibility, his animosity, his delusions. It finally occurred to me that being with him was not such a good idea. I told him my decision as we sat outside my friends' apartment, staring at each other awkwardly. "I don't want to date you anymore." Flat, to the point.

"Why not? Elizabeth, we're meant for each other. I went to jail for you!"

"You went to jail for shoplifting."

"But I love you!"

"I'm sorry. This just won't work out." I stayed firm. When he realized he couldn't talk me out of it, he began to cry. Softly at first, but when I didn't respond he began to howl and beat his fists on the grass. I watched with detachment as he flailed around, refusing to give him the attention he craved.

"Why? Why, God, why? Oh, the pain! My heart! The pain! I'm dying!" It occurred to me to suggest that he pray to the demon lord Mygara to spare his life, but I bit my tongue. He was getting pretty loud, and I started to be concerned.

"Really, are you okay? What hurts?" He didn't answer, just rolled in the grass, clutching his stomach and moaning. "Come on, Max. Get up."

"Ohhhh . . . God! I can see it! The tunnel . . . the light!" By this time my friends inside were getting alarmed. One of them offered to drive Max to the emergency room, though Max insisted it was probably too late. "My life, it's leaking away! Oh, the pain!" They hauled him off to the hospital, supporting him as he staggered, doubled over, to the car. He returned a few hours later, pushing past me to the room he slept in and slamming the door. I got the details from my friend.

"The doctor said his ulcer was aggravated. He gave Max some Tums."

After that I only saw Max on rare occasions. I stopped going to his hangouts, and he estranged himself from my friends after refusing to pay back the bail money he owed. He surfaced a few times to harass me when he heard I was dating someone new, and for a while he would mysteriously appear on my bus to call me a cold-hearted strumpet, or worse, to make small talk. One day I found a note stuck under a rock at my front door. It read:

> *Elizabeth. I am sorry things between us had to end as they did. I will always remember you and hold our time together dear in my heart. I hope you have a good life and that you find what your soul craves.*
>
> *Sincerely,*
> *Max*

*P.S. I changed the location of my buried treasure,
so don't go looking for it.*

That was the last I heard of him. Eventually I stopped visiting the area where he lived and lost touch with my friends who still kept in contact with him. I started a new life, one devoid of role-playing, melodrama and archnemeses. I still think about Max sometimes, and I realize now that he was a better vampire than I thought, because he sucked away a good three months of my life. I half-expect that one day he'll show up at my apartment in a suit of armor to tell me he never stopped loving me. But I conjure up memories of him now mostly to amuse myself. And it works.

Bad Date

Alison Luterman

T rying to talk with this man is
   like trying to drive through a blizzard:
My hands grip the steering wheel grimly.
My eyes are searchlights, peering through permafrost,
looking for a road somewhere out of the storm of his words.
The wheels keep slipping,
threatening to strand us somewhere in the middle of
a drift.
I can't see two feet in front of his argument,
I don't even know

what he's arguing about, now he seems to be smiling
as if he thought I agreed with him—
Don't panic!

Times like these, I miss my ex-husband.
I miss every man I ever had a reasonable conversation with.
I miss silence.

Being alone with this guy's thoughts
is like being on a squash court
with that vicious little ball bouncing off
the walls floor ceiling everywhere.

The waitress in the beautiful sari
has refilled our water glasses three times
but he doesn't feel he should leave a tip
because they didn't display their sign boldly enough outside.
He walked past three times, looking for the place.
He has asked to speak to the manager.

What's it like to be this guy?
Be in his head, I mean.

Talking to him, I feel like a frozen mouse,
about to be fed to a child's pet snake.
We have discussed my work and his work and agreed we both
   do Important Things.
We have talked about yoga, and meditation, and politics, and,
   god help us,
therapy.
First thing tomorrow, I will run away and join the circus.

Will I ever be with a man again like
   water braiding itself with water,
unconcerned as it whispers against wet stones?
Will it ever be that dance again, simple and
mysterious as laughter
arising from nowhere, arising from the belly in wordless warm
waves?

Now he has taken a deep breath
   and looked moistly into my eyes.
I think that means I am responsible for
   his emotional well-being

Bad Date

He is getting ready to recite
one of his poems. Maybe there will be an earthquake
and the chandelier will fall on our heads and I'll be spared.
Maybe a madman
will come in brandishing a gun and hold up this restaurant,
and I'll scream, "Guido! What took you so long?" and launch
    myself into his
arms, and the getaway car will be parked outside, idling.

Evolution

Vy Rhodes

Valentine's Day was creeping up far too quickly for my taste. I had been single for what seemed like decades, and I was determined not to let one more official holiday of romance slip by without a date. So I agreed to meet Ryan on February 14.

We'd "met" through a personals ad and had been corresponding for a couple of weeks. He was smart, polite and didn't reek of desperation. I'd already seen his picture, and it was downright charming—not the sort of fellow you expect to find in the personals. Then again, I'd never thought of myself as the type of woman who responds to personals ads.

A movie, a "meet my friends" dinner, a video at home—we

went through all of the required new-relationship steps. I was attracted to Ryan, even more so than I expected from the photo. He was a techie in his late twenties with a respectable job, a nice circle of friends and a pristine apartment. We did our share of kissing and went as far as partial nudity, but remained at a safe distance from the "promised land." The buildup was . . . building.

Ryan was such a romantic. He sent me mushy cards and emails, called just to say, "I'm thinking of you," and actually wanted to talk about our feelings ad nauseam. He was attentive, caring, sensitive—all the things that I, a modern woman, was supposed to want.

He ushered spiders out the door rather than squashing them with his bare hands. He actually cooked meals for his pampered little yappy dog; it was simply adorable. So why did it make me want to roll my eyes?

He'd call me right after work, often to ask me what happened on *Jenny Jones* that day. Gosh, how he loved those reuniting-family-member shows—we had so much in common!

I mused to myself that though Ryan was "supposed" to watch *The Sopranos* and ESPN and *Cops*, I had procured a rare specimen: an evolved man. So why did it bug me that he refused to burp out loud occasionally and leave damp towels on the bed? My eye-rolling told me that some part of me wasn't buying it. I felt adrift somehow. I couldn't believe it. There I was, missing damp towels and belching. Was I warped? Maybe. But it was true: I slowly came to realize that I favored even the gross "guy behavior" over this feminized version of manhood any day. I missed maleness: the yang to my yin, the sun to my moon, all of the clichéd, black-and-white gender comparisons we've heard before.

I began to feel sorry for Ryan. My, *that's* sexy.

The poor man, I thought. Another victim of the demasculinization movement of the 1990s. We've taught our men too well; we've told them they're supposed to cry, get in touch with their feelings, do laundry and write sappy poetry. We've told them to get rid of everything that makes them men.

Role delineation is important to me, though I guess I never knew it until I met Ryan. I wanted to be the girl! When I was scared to go to the dentist, I wanted my big, strong man to hold my hand. I didn't want to have to hold his. When something went "bump" in the night, the last thing I needed was a shivering lump under the covers encouraging me to ignore it and hope it would go away.

But how could I be so heartless? Here was a man coming to me with his heart oozing all over the place, doing everything possible to romance me. Maybe I could work on his masculinity. Maybe I could slip some power tools into his stylish wicker home-decorating-magazine baskets when he wasn't looking.

I was starting to wonder . . .

"Don't you ever get gas?" I asked him, and even as I said it, I understood the confused expression on his face. I was confusing myself, too. Maybe this was an identity crisis. Maybe tomorrow, I would wake up wishing he'd forget to flush the toilet.

"Umm, sure," he said, with that upward lilt in his voice that signifies a question rather than a statement.

"Do you just hold it in when I'm around?"

"I don't know," he said. "I guess I go to the bathroom."

"Why?"

"Why?" He repeated, now staring at me as if I had just asked him to eat a soil sandwich.

"Never mind," I mumbled. Trying to convince a guy to expel gas in front of you is probably a weird endeavor. After all, if he actually did it, I'd complain.

But, wait. Maybe that was just it. Maybe I needed something to complain about. Maybe I missed all of the past ogres in my life, who needed my gentle prodding to remind them to eat with utensils and use fabric softener.

Ryan had given me more home remedy tips than my own mother. I already knew that seltzer takes out stains, but it was news to me that mayonnaise makes an excellent monthly cream rinse. Why did he know these things?

Sisters. That was the inevitable answer. Still, it made me a little uncomfortable. He was a better woman than I was. He knew when JCPenney was having a sale on bathing suits, he ironed better than I did, and he got mistier at that antidrug commercial where the announcer says, "This is for all the kids who take the long way home from school."

And if he asked me if I wanted to talk about my feelings one more time . . . !

I wanted a man who would stick to being a man and let me be the woman. I wanted someone who would carry heavy stuff into the house for me, and change the oil on my car and light bulbs in my bedroom.

It wasn't his fault, really. He was just following instructions, like so many of the modern men we women claim to adore. He was listening to the women in his life, who had been telling him to be a "sensitive man" since toddlerhood. And, decidedly, it was as much my fault as anyone's. Sure, I'd yelled at past boyfriends, urging them to be more understanding and kind and neat and conscious of their color-scheme choices. But I hadn't really meant it. I'd just wanted to have a job in the relationship.

Now that Ryan had appeared on the scene, I saw the error of my ways. This was the future. If I continued to complain effectively, all the men in my path would turn into these ambiguously gendered people with hormone swings and an inability to mow lawns.

So, where did that leave me? How would I convince this guy to be a caveman again, so I could nag him about his caveman ways? It was impossible. *Out of mercy for his sanity, I should set him free,* I tepidly thought, not really wanting to go through with it. And then came the final straw.

There we were, steaming up the windows, hands running amok, when he turned to me and softly said, "I just want to hold you all night."

What?

It threw my sex drive into "park." I just couldn't take it anymore. To whom can we turn when our trusted boyfriends utter anticlimactic words like, "I just want to hold you all night"?

I mean, what's an appropriate response? "Thanks, but I'd prefer a quick and sweaty romp, closely followed by your departure so I can sleep without your snoring face on my pillow"?

Oh, come on. This wasn't love. Not for me. I found it impossible to fall in love with a man who watches the Lifetime channel. I just didn't need that kind of competition for the Girlfriend of the Year award.

As the female in the relationship, it was my duty to be the narcissistic, sensitive, weepy, maternal, fashion-conscious, coupon-clipping person with too many shoes. And somehow, my role had been usurped. Well, this relationship wasn't big enough for both of us. One of us had to leave.

It's probably more difficult to break up with a sensitive man than any other kind of person. He'd done absolutely nothing offensive or objectively wrong. There had been no beatings, no cheatings, no fights, no uncaring behaviors. And no matter what I might say, he would see the dumping as the result of Nice Guy Syndrome.

And that wasn't entirely accurate. I liked nice guys. I just wanted a nice guy who belched once in a while. Next time, I vowed, I was only going to nag lightly about the gross-guy behaviors. Enough to complete my required complaining quota, but not enough to induce any change.

So, I told him. At the end of our "I just want to hold you" date, I told him that the sparks just weren't there for me, and I didn't see a future to the relationship. I added the obligatory "but I still want to be friends" line, and I meant it, too. He was a good shopping buddy. Who else would tell me if those pumps clashed with my pocketbook?

He cried.

Of course he cried. Couldn't you see that coming? He cried for what seemed like weeks. He came over to my house simply to cry. "Closure," he said, and I cursed Oprah.

I needed to point out to him that his mourning period had lasted longer than our relationship had. I couldn't stand the guilt anymore. I had broken a sensitive man's heart, and no matter how many good deeds I committed from now on, that was always going to be a black mark on my permanent record.

I imagined him back in his Martha Stewart–inspired apartment with the immaculate bathroom and tasteful upholstery. I pictured him crying into his down pillow, wondering what he had done wrong. "If only I had belched once or twice," he'd wail.

And, somehow, that was exactly the image I used to rationalize my guilt: He had stolen my coping mechanisms. It wasn't bad enough that he was better at cooking and grooming and finding low-fat snacks. Nooo. He had to be better at wallowing in heartbreak, too. He had pushed the line too far. It was no longer my job to help him.

As for me, I coped the only logical way I could: with porn, sports bars and fast cars. Hey, someone had to.

The Reluctant Goddess

Zonna

I knew right from the beginning that it would be a bad idea to go anywhere near Carrie. In fact, if you look up the word "mistake" in certain dictionaries, you'll see a picture of the two of us in a circle with a big red line through it. We'd been casual friends for a few years. She knew I was gay; I knew she wasn't. It had never been an issue before. We'd still been able to eat lunch together, laugh and swap stories of past conquests, trying to make each other blush.

Then one night, as we were sitting in her car by the lake, just hanging out and skipping stones from the window and watching the ripples radiate, Carrie tossed in a boulder. She confessed that she was deeply in love with me and had been for nearly a year. She said she wasn't physically attracted to women in general, but there was something about me specifically that intoxicated her. It wasn't just a crush, she promised. It wasn't curiosity or a mere affection sprouting from the fertile soil of familiarity. She was drawn to love me—compelled. Even if she had wanted to stop herself, she would not have been able. I was amazing, she said, a marvel. The world was blessed because I existed. She loved everything to do with me: loved thinking of me, loved talking with me, loved being near me, loved even the thought itself of loving me. Love, love, love, love, love!

But as pure and holy as her feelings were, they were not simply ethereal. Maybe it was the smoky sound of my voice, she conjectured, that set her loins on fire; or perhaps it was the way I moved, or the light in my eyes. Whatever the reason, she thought about me all the time—usually naked. She admitted she knew I didn't feel the same about her, but said she wanted to "give herself" to me anyway.

I was flattered, of course, and a little embarrassed. How does one respond to such an offer? Mostly, though, I was stunned. I hadn't seen it coming. Maybe I should have. Maybe I hadn't been paying enough attention. But really, even if I had examined our relationship under an electron microscope, how could I have ever expected to find this crawling around in the petri dish? She was straight. Did I mention that? Straight, as in squeamish enough to giggle and cover her eyes if a movie included any girl-on-girl action. Straight, as in not understanding what two women could possibly do in bed together, besides sleep. And, oh yeah—straight, as in married.

Yes, she was married; yes, to a man. I know, I know . . . it was a bad idea. Hooking up with a straight woman was foolish enough, but a married one—why, it defied one of the most basic lesbian commandments: "Thou shalt not even consider getting involved with a married woman unless thou looketh for big trouble." And she was definitely married. They'd been together for close to fifteen years. She said she loved her husband. This had nothing to do with him, she assured me. This was about her and me and destiny. It was larger than life. Bigger than both of us. An undeniable attraction she simply had to act on. She'd kept it to herself for far too long; now she wanted to give it to me.

I remember thinking, Is this a common occurrence? Do all heterosexual women behave this way, given the opportunity? Do lesbians hold some secret erotic power over straight women? Is it just a matter of proximity and timing? Look at Ellen and Anne, or Melissa and Julie. Had this phenomenon been covered in Lesbian 101 on a day I skipped class?

As I sat in the car, inches away from the lips that wanted so badly to be pressed against my own, I tried to process the information. No matter how I looked at it, the facts remained the same. She was married, and she wanted to sacrifice her hetero-sexuality to me as an act of adulation because she was so in love with me. Maybe I should have been more prepared for her epiphany, or maybe that was impossible. Either way, I knew this was a rocky road, and not a path I'd ever considered. I didn't want to be idolized. I didn't have the right shoes.

I tried to be kind. I said no—no you're not, no I can't, no thanks.

She called me every day from work for two weeks to see if I'd changed my mind. Sometimes she called me twice in the same afternoon, as if those three hours that had passed since her last inquiry had contained the difference between no and yes, as if she didn't want to miss the very moment when the sky lit up and I sanctified her desire. Our covenant would be glo-rious, she predicted. It would be heavenly. It would be conven-ient. She presented many convincing arguments, including her willingness to "try anything," as if that phrase, in and of itself, was a particularly tempting sexual act.

I tried to be firm. I said no—no way, no chance, no good.

She wrote me pages and pages of beautiful poetry filled with sensuous images of how it would be if we made love and mystical references to the past lives we'd already shared. In touch with her spiritual side, she was sure we'd been lovers in a previous incarnation. She said she was destined to search for my soul over and over until we were joined once again. It was her mission to love me. It was written on her heart. I should let her fulfill the prophecy so that she could move on to the next level.

I tried to resist. I said no—no past, no future, no point.

She showed up unannounced at my back door in the middle of a sunny afternoon wearing nothing but a long, flowing silk robe with buttons from head to toe—all undone.

The passion play lasted only one season.

It was a very hot summer. Although she claimed to have been intoxicated, it was I who was seduced. Everything about her turned me on: the way she smiled (slow, like a blossoming flower), the way she laughed at my jokes (without hesitation, like a sudden gust of wind), the way she worried about me all the time (Are you eating right? I made you some soup. Do you feel tired? Here, I brought vitamins). She worshipped me. She was devoted. I was a goddess.

And like a goddess, I benevolently bestowed favors upon my disciples, of which she was the only one. I took what she gave me, accepting her sacrifices greedily, and in return I shared with her the many carnal secrets I'd learned. In short, I made her squeal with delight.

Many were the nights when she'd sneak away from her unsuspecting husband to worship at my altar. She gave herself up entirely, allowing me to do as I wished with her. She was always appreciative of my attentions and voiced her passion in no uncertain terms. Easily aroused, her skin melted at my touch, becoming instantly pliant and responsive. She trembled and moaned when I teased her, making me eager to bestow more blessings on her until she cried out my name in ecstasy as she caught a glimpse of nirvana. I admit it was exciting to think my charms had lured this exquisite beauty from the arms of a man. My head swelled to such proportions I could scarcely fit through the door. I really was amazing. Who but a goddess could possibly command such power over another human being?

I would see her three, maybe four times a week, whenever

she could manage to get away. She anticipated my every need. She cooked me sumptuous meals and fed them to me with her fingers. She planted flowers in my yard so I could enjoy their beauty when hers wasn't readily available. She let me sleep late, tiptoeing around so as not to disturb me, waiting patiently for me to awaken. She cleaned my house while I relaxed and read the paper (a goddess needs to keep up on things, you know). She shaved my legs. She washed my hair. She picked up my groceries, waxed my car, ran numerous errands for me, and even answered the telephone so I wouldn't have to talk to any annoying telemarketers. All this she did with a cheerful attitude, acting as though I was granting her the ultimate benediction by allowing her to cater to my every whim.

And oh, but my little zealot was full of surprises. Her creativity was boundless. As she'd promised, there was nothing she wouldn't try. Each day brought a new benefaction, as she entertained me with sensuous dances and titillating costumes designed to maintain a constant state of stimulation. My bureau was overflowing with sexual aids she'd ordered in my name from various catalogs: vibrators, dildos, body paints, blindfolds, plugs, paddles, restraints . . . . (Good Vibrations mailed me a thank-you card embossed in gold. Eve's Garden sent me a plaque.) She was a good student too, learning quickly how to please me. One would never have guessed that she was new to the faith. What she lacked in knowledge, she more than made up for with enthusiasm. She spent hours learning every inch of my body until she knew each line, each curve, each freckle by heart. Her fingers memorized my erogenous zones. I would quiver at the mere sight of her tongue, knowing what it was capable of. I was dizzy from so much pleasure. Indeed, I was a happy goddess, starting to feel glad I had baptized her after all.

Time flew by and soon the summer was winding down. As the leaves changed color, so did she. The transformation began gradually, at first almost imperceptibly: a less than zealous look in her eyes; an apathetic response to a suggestion that would have previously elicited fervor. In the beginning, she had been satisfied simply to sit at my feet and bask in my glow; now she wanted to adjust the temperature. It seemed she needed more and more from me. Perhaps I should have been able to predict this. Religion, like any other mind-altering drug, can be addictive. Apostles and junkies are cut from the same piece of cloth, after all—one from the center and one from the edge.

I was gripped by a nagging feeling, as if I'd forgotten something very important. Atop my mountain, with my head enveloped in clouds, I had been so caught up in my own PR that I had failed to recognize the familiar pattern as it unfolded: date, mate, regulate.

It wasn't long before everything about her turned me off: the way she smiled (too slowly, like she couldn't quite commit), the way she laughed at my jokes (without humor, like a dry cough), the way she worried all the time (Are you eating too much? You look fat. Are you tired of me? What have I done besides love you?). She still worshipped me. I was a goddess, after all, and she could only hope to be fashioned in my image—but she had some ideas for improvements.

First, she wanted to change me.

I really shouldn't eat meat, she said, it wasn't good for me. She gave me macrobiotic cookbooks. (In my religion, the word "tofu" is blasphemous.) She dragged me to vegetarian restaurants with pristine grills that had never seen a hamburger. She emptied my refrigerator while I was out (at McDonald's) and filled it with green leafy things, unnatural juice combinations and EggBeaters.

I really should get more exercise, she advised, and took me

on long walks in secluded areas where I couldn't hitchhike back to the car. At night she anointed my constantly cramping leg muscles with strange-smelling oils.

I really needed to take better care of myself, she warned, and made unwanted appointments for me with massage therapists, Reiki masters and suspiciously thin nutritionists. I am not now, nor have I ever been, what one might call svelte. Goddesses are supposed to be larger than life, anyway.

Next, she wanted to swallow me.

Everywhere I turned, there she was. Even when we hadn't made a date she would (in)conveniently show up wherever I happened to be, expanding her role as follower to new dimensions. I wondered if her husband ever suspected where she was and what she was doing, or if he was simply relieved to find her missing. She went from hanging on my every word to hanging all over me. She always wanted to hold my hand, or sit too close. More than once, I found myself reaching for my inhaler, except I didn't own one. Even when the weather started to cool, I felt too warm around her. A goddess needs her space, after all.

Finally, she wanted to be me.

She began dressing like I did, exchanging her polyester pantsuits for jeans and flannel shirts. She cut her hair in the same style. It was strange to look at her. I wondered if Moses felt the same way when he saw Charlton Heston.

She quoted me—not anything profound I might have said, just everyday statements gleaned from casual conversations. She adopted my cadence when she spoke, and interjected my favorite expressions into her own dialogues. If a friend called while she was alone at my house, she pretended to be me, often convincingly. I would find out days later when confronted about something I had allegedly said or promised.

Finally, she discarded her last name, as I had long ago, and began introducing herself as "just Carrie." That was frightening. The novice was finally a full-fledged lesbian. Unfortunately, she had been too good a student, and I had taught her much too well. Not only had she learned all the commandments, but also how to break them. In a short time, she had mastered all the little quirks and annoying habits of every past girlfriend I'd ever had. My part-time worries became full-time fears. I took to pinching myself for confirmation that I still existed. The bruises took on a divine significance, like stigmata. One day, I looked at myself in the mirror (the real one, not the counterfeit one that walked and talked and borrowed my clothes). I looked terrible. The burden of living up to her veneration had taken its toll on me. If this is what being a goddess entailed, I was ready to hand in my resignation. No exit interview necessary.

As far as I was concerned, it was over, except for the details. I just needed to end it. I was not a vengeful goddess, and I didn't want to hurt Carrie's feelings, but I was getting too uncomfortable. I tried to think of ways to allow her to figure it out for herself. I prayed for a revelation. That way she could hold on to her pride. That way she could pretend it was her idea. That way I could avoid a scene. I may have been a goddess, but I was also a chicken. I wondered if other deities had encountered similar problems.

I processed and processed, giving myself a goddess-sized headache. In the end, though, I didn't have to devise any elaborate scheme at all. Like every other girlfriend I'd ever had, she eventually grew tired of me and left. If I had been a real goddess, I suppose I would have been able to predict that.

And so ends this tale. There's probably a moral to this story, but since I am no longer a goddess, it's not my responsibility to tell you what it is.

Money Shot

Michelle Goodman

Some people go cold turkey half a dozen times before they finally swear off cigarettes or bourbon or cocaine. With me, it was one-night stands.

It wasn't that I'd had more short-lived trysts than most. I hadn't. Sure, between the green-haired barista I screwed in the storeroom, the street punk I fondled in the furniture warehouse he called home and the barely legal river guide I topped in the tent, I'd had a record-setting season of sordidness. But when it came to the morning—no, the hour—after cheap sex, I caught myself muttering the words "never again" with alarming frequency. A couple of weeks later, though, I'd be at a bar or a party or a café, and a strapping young lad would catch my eye, once again quashing my dreams of living a pure and chaste existence.

Maybe it was because I'd spent the better part of my twenties festering in a sad excuse for a live-in relationship and needed to kick up some dust. Or because I stupidly thought lust and intimacy didn't, or maybe couldn't, coexist. Or because I kidded myself that some semblance of a sex life, no matter how meaningless, was better than none at all.

At any rate, I have the Love@AOL portal, the one with the perky little red heart icon, to thank for helping me kick the cheap-sex habit. That's where I met Phil, the guy who compelled me to swear off one-night love for good.

Phil was one of about 197 men who answered the online ad I placed when I decided I was ready again for a Relationship—at least, a relationship of sorts. I wasn't looking for a life partner, and I didn't want just one night either; I wanted a guy with whom I could enjoy stripping down and, afterward, actually conversing—and maybe even repeating this process, possibly for weeks on end.

Most men responded with form letters about sunset walks and breaking waves. Some revealed the intimate details of their stock portfolios or mental health issues. Others casually dropped phrases like, "someone I can build a family with" or "doggie style" in the first sentence of their letters. I was in grave danger of wearing out my Delete button.

Phil's emails were the antithesis of the trite love poems and wife-hunting missives crowding my mailbox. For one thing, he could spell. For another, he knew how to locate his sense of humor, and he wasn't one to cower from my sarcastic jabs. We quickly escalated to instant messaging.

I can't remember exactly what Phil and I talked about, or if we had anything in common besides the desire to get naked, but his corny quips had me spitting my root beer all over the keyboard. I'd type, "How are you?" and he'd respond, "From what I hear, fantastic. Let me come over tonight, and I'll show you."

Though I griped and groaned about all his locker-room innuendoes, truth be told, I ate it up. Maybe because he was the first cyberdate I'd encountered with an intellect, a shred of personality. Maybe because I worked at home and had only the FedEx and UPS deliverymen for company. Or maybe because I was a masochist.

Phil wanted to meet me right away. I stalled for a week though, not ready for the cyberlust to come crashing to its cruel, inevitable halt. I pretty much expected that, like the handful of other cyberdates I'd met in person, he'd disappoint—be it his distracting nervous tics, unfortunate sense of hygiene or remarkable knack for self-loathing.

The flesh-and-blood Phil had none of these problems. He made me laugh even harder. As a bonus, he seemed to have no trouble stringing together eight sentences in a row, and I could almost see myself letting him suck on my nipples.

Phil was geeky—not computer geeky like me, but exercise-freak, sales-guy geeky. He was foxy, but not the kind of stone-cold fox that usually stops me in my tracks. His dark hair was short, crisp and so gelled that any movement was out of the question. I could easily see him at a telecommunications trade show, bathed in aftershave, clad in pleated khakis and a white oxford with a little horse on the chest.

Phil's tight white T-shirt showed off his swollen biceps, and a thin gold chain peeked out of his collar. He could have been the poster child for Nautilus gym equipment, his indiscreet muscles begging for adulation. I envisioned him at the gym in a unitard, on his back, wearing one of those ridiculous body-building belts, buried under an impossibly enormous barbell.

Yet spending hours on end giggling in instant chats with

someone changes your perspective on what your "type" is and isn't. So what if he resembles a corporate raider and doesn't have any squishy body parts? So what if he looks like the breed of guy you usually saw strolling through Pacific Heights, arm in arm with a Banana Republic–clad blond who's wearing a suede jacket and sandals—in winter.

Phil met me at my apartment, which, according to a friend who ate, slept and shat *The Rules,* was a no-no. As we guzzled the bottle of pricey merlot he'd brought (another no-no), we made that nauseatingly clever small talk people make when they're trying to sound smart, or at least different from everyone else. Most likely, we dissed people who catalog-shopped and obsessed about home furnishings. And we probably ticked off our international travel wish lists and casually recommended to each other political magazines we hadn't read in years. I'm certain, though, that we abandoned all illusions of making it to our eight o'clock dinner reservations.

A couple of hours after his arrival, the wine was gone and Phil's head lay balanced in my lap, his half-sotted pupils staring up at me. At which point he asked me what I thought of him. It was a question to which I didn't feel equipped to respond.

As I pondered what to say, he sat up to kiss my neck. Unable to count on one hand how many months it had been since my last tumble, I said nothing and instead nibbled on his lips. A nanosecond later, he was standing before me wearing nothing but his socks. He triumphantly placed one foot on the couch—like he was posing for an Eddie Bauer catalog, but in the nude.

His socks, which were pulled halfway up his sculpted calves, were dark and pinstriped, the kind you see poking out from under the slacks of guys who wear ties every day. I blinked dumbly. Did I miss something? Where the hell did his clothes go? It was as though he'd stepped into a phone booth, spun around like Clark Kent and come out naked.

It occurred to me that perhaps he executed this routine on a somewhat regular basis. It also occurred to me that he might have a wife and kids, a live-in boyfriend, a penknife clenched in his ass. Rather than ask or obsess, I took a mental inventory of the supplies my nightstand housed: a box of heavy-duty condoms, a can of pepper spray and a telephone with 911 set on autodial.

"Aren't you going to say anything about how big it is?" he inquired, nodding down to the place where his boxers had been just moments ago. I was so stunned by his disrobing that I hadn't even had a chance to notice the size of the thing.

Somehow, I managed not to laugh. I considered asking him and his hard-on to show themselves out. But first I decided to sneak a peek.

Suddenly, the whole living room seemed to be filled with his nakedness, his dick quickly ballooning to one hundred times its size. I had to admit, it was impressive. I nonchalantly offered the compliment he was so absurdly trolling for. I figured, what the hell, and began tugging at my blouse.

My apartment had a long, skinny hallway with a door-sized mirror on either end. Within minutes, we'd maneuvered ourselves from the couch to the hall, with me pressed between Phil's hard-on and the wall. As Phil worked my breasts and kissed me hard without opening his mouth, he spastically grinned, swiveling his head first to the left, then to the right, so he could admire both naked reflections of himself. I was reminded of a dog sandwiched between a cat and a gravy-basted bone, baffled as to which to stare at—much less, consume—first. The front door and my bedroom were equidistant from where we stood groping. I contemplated my options; Phil marveled at his mirror images.

I've never been one to walk out on a movie, no matter how uninspiring, and I make myself read every book I start from cover to cover. You can see where I'm going with this. I had to know, had to follow through with this escapade, even if just to satisfy my sheer curiosity. And so I led him to my bed.

He placed a finger on the space between my legs. "Fast or slow?" he asked plainly, clinically, as though inquiring whether I wanted soup or salad. Coffee or tea. Paper or plastic.

"Slow," I replied, wondering how frequently he asked that question, and of how many women. And how many women opted for "fast" right out of the gates.

Then: "One finger or two?"

It was like being at a McDonald's drive-thru. *Two please, and no, I do not want fries with that. Yes, to go.*

Petting and probing soon led to penetration, but not before he bitched and moaned at my insistence on a condom. After giving him the verbal equivalent of a slap upside the head, I quickly climbed on top. Which is when Phil went into porn-star-wannabe overdrive.

"Oooh, you ride me so good baby."

How does one respond to such a statement? *Uh, thanks. Giddyup.*

"Let me come on your face. I want to come on your face," he cooed.

Yeah, and I want you to put your tongue in my mouth and between my legs, but that doesn't seem to be happening either.

More whining about the latex oppression of his prick, and in a flash he was out of me, despite the fact that I was not ready for him to abandon ship. He knelt at the foot of the bed, holding the limp condom in his left hand and fondling his swollen piece with his right.

I stared in disbelief as he proceeded to finish himself off, his chunky silver watchband rising and falling with every wheezing breath. Usually the sight of a guy doing himself, in my bed no less, had me moaning within three seconds. But the show this guy was putting on didn't ring true: It had Meg Ryan written all over it.

His head thrashed wildly, his hips ground the air faster and faster, and he yelped like an injured pup. For at least five minutes. Maybe six.

I imagined him doing this before a full-length mirror at home each morning. His desire seemed fueled only by his ample rod, which he stroked lovingly from balls to tip, not missing an inch, admiring his unit the entire time. For him, I could have been anyone. I could have been asleep. I could have not even been in the room. Part of me wished that were the case.

When he shot his load, it of course didn't arrive in a neat puddle or dribble; it was a frigging jet stream, a lawn sprinkler hitting every blade of grass in the yard. And it was headed my way.

Since I hadn't seen his health records, I angled my head to avoid catching some of the fast-approaching tsunami in my mouth and eyes. Oh, he was a good shot all right. Despite my tuck and roll, he managed to hit his mark, to shower my neck and chin with fluid, from five feet away. When he got up to leave, claiming "Big day tomorrow," I was hardly disappointed.

I could now scratch "visit the set of an adult film" off the list of things I thought it would be interesting to do once before I died. In a small way, I felt like I'd witnessed a carnal thespian in all his contrived, fetishized, impersonalized glory—money shot and all.

The morning after my three-hour "date" with Phil, I dubbed him Telephone Dick. I called a friend who I knew didn't keep a copy of *The Rules* under her pillow and complained that my cervix was painfully spasming and that I had begun fantasizing about spending the day in the emergency room.

"What? Was he huge or something?" my friend excitedly asked.

"Kind of. He was as big as my telephone," was my dazed reply.

"I don't know about you, but my telephone must be about ten inches long and I don't even want to know how wide," she laughed. "You might want to take it a little slower next time you see ol' Telephone Dick," she said, adding, "you lucky ho."

Doubled over and growing more fetal by the minute, I knew I'd sooner take a vow of celibacy than have a "next time" with T.D.

As I clutched a heating pad against my belly, I swore off personals ads, cyberchats, blind dates, one-night flings and any other dating evil I could think of. I cancelled my AOL account and promised myself that next time I met a man, it would be on a plane, in a bookstore, at the gas station—somewhere we could sniff each other out, face to face. Get to know each other first. Become friends, then lovers. Like normal people do, those without email accounts anyway.

I didn't answer the phone for a week, fearing it might be T.D. coming after me with his telephone-sized member. T.D. didn't seem to mind that I never picked up, and left me messages for six days straight. "What do you expect? You practically gave it up for free!" cried my *Rules* friend, with whom I'd made the mistake of sharing far too many details.

I've often been called a woman of extremes when it comes to

my relations with men. I'm like a pendulum, swinging from one end of the spectrum to the other. In many ways, I remained true to pattern after meeting Phil.

Not only did I kick meaningless trysts once and for all, the next time I met a guy, I fell in love. And to my unending delight, my new love's jimmy was scarcely bigger than my index finger.

Haiku

A. C. Hall

I break up with him.
In surprise, he drops his mug.
He says, "My coffee!"

Big Dyke on Campus

Megan Lambert

I am not a lesbian. But I'm not straight either. So let's call me . . . bisexual—even though that word makes me feel cut in half on bad days and trampy on good ones. "Dyke" will do, too, or "queer," I guess . . . Anyway, I promise this is more than a standard coming-out saga: I won't get into the messy details of coming out to my family, chopping off my hair and attending women's rugby games. Instead, let's focus on the good stuff: dyke drama à la my alma mater, Smith College, Northampton, Massachusetts, Lesbianville, U.S.A., the Earth, right next door to Venus, spinning away through space and time.

Throughout my adolescence, I quietly questioned my sexuality.

Actually, this questioning was utterly silent and in my own head, except for a few tentative and very brief conversations with other high school friends who have since come flaming out of quite a few closets themselves—according to my hometown's ever churning rumor mill. But, despite my undeniable teenage attraction to members of my own sex, I felt unable to take on the lesbian mantle, even after arriving at Smith College and attending a number of shirts-optional LBA (Lesbian Bisexual Association) dances. I was, after all, quite attracted to boys too, and my Catholic and fundamentalist Christian family could barely handle that. When I was about thirteen, my mother amended her pre-puberty statement, "You can talk to me about anything," with phrases like, "Don't get married until you are at least thirty," "Don't have sex before you are married" and "Gay people are unnatural." (She's come a long way since then.)

So, when I found myself in my second year of college utterly single and madly in love with my friend—let's call her Eva— while simultaneously attracted to guys, I felt a bit messed up, to say the least. Eva was a first-year student (there were and are no fresh*men* at Smith College), and the slope of her cheekbones drove me to distraction. But alas, even if I had been in the state of mind to embrace my sexuality and then try to embrace hers, Eva had a boyfriend—let's call him Barry. And though I occasionally mustered up the courage to admit my sexual attraction without regard to gender, I just wasn't gettin' any.

It did not help matters that my roommate—let's call her Holly—was an aspiring BDOC (Big Dyke on Campus). She routinely skipped classes to have sex all day in our room with whomever she was dating at the time and often carried on with these activities while I was "asleep" in my bed at night. Holly also had the charming propensity to make loud proclamations like, "Oh Megan, you are so straight!" to distinguish her dykier-than-thou self from me. Granted, I did talk an awful lot about how much I enjoyed sex with boys. I was grossly explicit in an effort to claim my tenuous hold on heterosexuality—especially whenever I was talking to Eva about sex. She, of all people, needed to know that I liked dick.

But I wasn't the only one talking. Eva told me sex stories as well. Usually they were about Barry and how sweet he was in bed. They called their favorite sexual position the "starfish," and even though I never quite figured out what it entailed, all I wanted was a big wave to come crashing down over Barry and send him out to sea. This was not a purely selfish desire. Barry was a creep. *He* had the charming propensity to utter statements like, "Poor Eva. I have to do all of the decision making in this relationship." Eva deserved better.

And even though Eva clung to her relationship with Barry for most of that school year, she began to look around a bit as she questioned her own sexuality. I told her that although I was sometimes curious about sex with women, I could never "experiment" with a woman because I would not want to objectify her and thus disrespect all of the *real lesbians* (like Holly?), who had to live with homophobia every day. Of course if, during one of those talks, Eva had suggested that she and I do some starfishing of our own, I would have jumped at the chance and jumped on her. But she never did. Instead, she formed a crush on a senior living in our house—an official BDOC no less— let's call her Autumn.

Autumn oozed charisma, dripped with sarcasm and Rollerbladed everywhere. She was an aspiring actress and writer and told sexually explicit jokes during Smith's traditional Thursday-night candlelight dinners. She got away with calling women "girls," wrote articles about women's porn for the school paper and was rumored to always fall for straight girls. Oh, and she was cute. Very. If I hadn't been so busy being jealous of her,

I would have wanted in her pants too. Listening to Eva go on about Autumn was pure torture. "You have a boyfriend!" I was shocked to hear myself say one night. What the hell was I doing defending Barry? Horrible, scummy, gets-to-starfish-with-Eva Barry?

After about three months of this, I decided that something had to be done. Because I was too chicken to try to seduce Eva and because I was too insecure about my attractiveness to any of the BDOCs, I decided to pursue the tried and true: boys. I set out on a mission to get laid, and although I was too much of a feminist to use a woman for such a purpose, I had no qualms whatsoever about using a guy. Of course, it was not so easy to meet guys at Smith. But then, one weekend, the a cappella singing group that Eva and I belonged to traveled to Brown University to sing with one of the men's groups there. In the audience was the brother of one of the Brown singers. I no longer even remember his name, so calling him Tom is not some sensitive effort to protect his identity in this totally unauthorized piece.

Tom was a *freshman* at Dartmouth. We sat next to each other on a couch at a post-concert party at someone's apartment. Given the events of the next few weeks, I would like to say that I was drinking that night, but I honestly don't remember. In any case, we talked politics. It was fall 1994, and we were both bemoaning Newt Gingrich's ascent to power. Tom was especially mournful because he was one of the few liberal voices at Dartmouth and felt isolated and appalled in the midst of keggers-for-conservatism and whatnot. At the end of the night, we exchanged email addresses in order to continue our political conversation, and I left the party to return to Smith with Eva and the rest of our singing group.

Over the next few weeks Tom and I emailed back and forth, daily notes filled with flirtatious quips, coy punctuation-based codes—;) :) :o—and political declarations that made my bleeding heart flutter. Before too long, he invited me to come visit him at Dartmouth. He wooed me with promises of a lecture by Angela Davis and ample opportunities to confront Republican bigots in his dorm. Of course, in my desperation, he also provided me with the chance to get laid and to get my mind off Eva starfishing with Barry and lusting after an official BDOC on Rollerblades. And so, condoms in bag, I boarded a bus bound for Dartmouth.

After a long bus ride, I had to take a shuttle van from the station. The van driver asked if I was a student at the university.

"No," I said. "I'm here to visit my boyfriend." Hopes were high at this point, you see. The driver dropped me off in front of the hotel where Tom said he would meet me, and told me to have fun. Determined to do just that, I went to a pay phone and dialed Tom's number. He said he'd be right over.

I stood in front of the hotel, looking out over the campus green, and then I saw someone coming across the grass toward me. My heart sank—or maybe it disappeared entirely, for I was quite heartless as I muttered to myself, "Please don't let that be him." Even from a distance I could tell that Tom was not going to be the answer to any of my hopes, except perhaps by defining to whom I was definitely not attracted. First of all, he was awfully short, and the shock of this made me realize that I had never seen him standing; he had remained seated throughout our post-concert political discussion, and all of our subsequent "conversations" had taken place over the Internet. I had dated plenty of below-average-height boys before, and at five foot four, I am no Amazon. But, for some reason, Tom's height, or lack thereof, was a problem.

So was his walk. He slouched and bounced along like a Muppet as he got closer and closer, and then there he was, beaming up at me. I realized that he'd been wearing a baseball cap at the party. He needed that baseball cap. It had covered up a truly unfortunate haircut, and it had somehow provided shadows to hide the asymmetrical look of his face. I don't mean to make Tom sound monstrous. I am sure that there are people out there who would find him attractive. The problem was, I definitely wasn't one of them, and this dashed my shallow hopes for the weekend. I was destined to return to Smith the following Monday without any raucous sex tales to share with the lovely, unattainable Eva, and in the meantime, I had to figure out how to deal with Tom, whose face showed no disappointment as he looked up at me and said, "Can I carry your bag?"

"No," I said quickly. I did not want him to do anything for me. I wanted to run down the road and catch up with that nice van driver man, screaming, "Take me with you! My prince has turned into a frog!"

But instead, I followed Tom back to his room. We talked politics a bit, I halfheartedly chastised his geeky roommate for the *Playboy* centerfolds hanging above his desk, and I made it very clear that I would not be sleeping with Tom in his bed. He offered to sleep on the floor, and I agreed that would be best.

That night, as I tried to drift off to sleep, dreaming of Eva and wearing a turtleneck and leggings, Tom said, "So, this isn't exactly what I thought would be happening tonight."

I sat bolt upright in bed and looked down at him on the floor. "What do you mean?" I asked defensively.

"Well," he started, "I'm just thinking that I could be kissing you right now."

Pause.

And then I said, "No, you couldn't be, because I don't want to kiss you."

That was the end of our conversation that night.

The next day, we walked around campus, got pizza and killed time until the Angela Davis lecture. Tom mustered up the courage to ask me, "So, why didn't you want to kiss me last night?" And from somewhere in the deep recesses of my shallow being, I offered up a feeble attempt at sensitivity, a virginal façade, a bold-faced lie: "I just don't go around kissing people," I said. "I'm sorry if you got the wrong idea about me."

This opened the door for Tom to analyze my reluctance to kiss him, my it's-not-you-it's-pure-little-old-me defense. "You are afraid of opening yourself up," he said. And I endured more, lots more, of this Psych 101 babble until the lecture that evening.

Angela Davis was brilliant, of course. But halfway through her lecture, all of the frat boys in the audience (this was Dartmouth after all) started booing her. I was appalled! I was horrified! I was given my out!

"You know, Tom," I said as we walked back to his dorm, "I think I want to head back to Smith tomorrow instead of waiting until Monday. I don't know how you manage to put up with all of the conservative jerks around here."

And so, the next morning we walked across the campus green together to wait for the shuttle to take me back to the bus station. I carried my bag, which still had the unopened box of condoms I had brought with me, and when my van arrived, I held the bag in front of me to avoid having to hug Tom goodbye.

"I'll email you," he said.

When I got back to Smith, Holly asked me how my weekend was. "Don't ask," I replied. "Dartmouth is a hellhole of conservatism, and I was a total bitch to the guy I was staying with just because he did not fit some image I didn't even know I had of the ideal guy."

"Yeah," said clueless Eva, who was also in the room. "I wondered what you saw in him."

During the spring semester, I made a few more failed hetero-sexual attempts to jump-start my love life. These included a boring two months with a guy whom I threw out of bed one night after he confessed that he was a registered Republican; a blasé one-night stand with a singer from BU who did nothing for me in bed; and a date with a guy who had what can only be described as bad lesbian hair. This last encounter was the closest I came to entering the world of dyke dating. It wasn't close enough. Meanwhile, Eva continued to alternately cling to Barry, pine away over Autumn and tell me all about both activities. But by the end of the school year, she had dumped Barry and experimented a little with girls. I saw my chance.

A few weeks later, while our singing group was in Switzerland, I drunkenly told Eva that I was in love with her. She held me and wisely told me that she was not in a place emotionally to do anything sexual. She also said that even if she hadn't just dumped her boyfriend of three years and hooked up with a woman for the first time, all in the past month, she valued our friendship too much to do anything that might risk it. "I need you as a friend, Megan," she said, and I was utterly humiliated.

I spent the remainder of our trip an absolute emotional wreck. She wasn't ready; I couldn't push her. Eva was gloriously patient and perfect in every way until I found her lying—in bed with another woman, early one morning before anyone else had awakened. It was evident that they had spent the night together. Let's call this other woman the Bane of My Existence. Dykier-than-thou to beat even Holly, prone to rattling off her fourteen hundred-plus SAT scores just for kicks, cocky about her truly lovely alto singing voice and known for cheating on her girlfriends, the Bane of My Existence was also petite, blond and blue-eyed. Most importantly, of course, she was in Eva's arms. I made a split-second assessment of the situation:

Were they fully clothed? (Yes.)

Had they kissed? (No way to know for sure.)

Slept together? (*No way to know for sure!*)

Did Eva actually think I was less attractive than the Bane of My Existence? (Apparently so. One thing about which I was absolutely certain was that I would never be blond, blue-eyed or petite.)

How much would a tell-all call to the Bane of My Existence's girlfriend back in Massachusetts cost?

Did Eva tell the Bane of My Existence about my proclamations of love? (Humiliation on top of heartbreak!)

And, what happened to the part about Eva not being ready for anything sexual?

No one said a word. I grabbed my towel and went to take a shower. Trying to block out the image of Eva lying on her bed in someone else's arms, I focused on my surroundings: The water was lukewarm; the spray was weak; someone had left long pieces of dark hair stuck to the white tile wall; the floor was grungy and I had no flip-flops.

I returned to the room, shivering, my hair wrapped in my towel. The Bane of My Existence was gone and Eva was putting on lip balm. Burt's Bees.

"So are you even going to speak to me?" she asked.

And this opened the door to the last conversation Eva and I would have about "us." She told me that nothing sexual had happened the previous night, and she said that even if something had happened, it would have been because she had nothing to lose with the Bane of My Existence. I chose to believe her. Sort of. And I resolved never to bring up my feelings for Eva again—at least not in a conversation with her. Other friends were fair game, and many a Smithie endured my tale of woe as I licked my wounds and got on with bi life. They indulged me with statements like, "You would have made a great couple!"; "She's insane to reject you!"; "I always knew you were a dyke."

And my favorite: "You are way more babelicious than the Bane of My Existence." Let's call the friend who said this . . . Angel.

But amidst all of this stroking of my poor wounded ego, no one ever did call me a BDOC. I lacked the butch appearance necessary for that status, not to mention I had yet to hook up with a woman. But that's another story.

Tonight I'm Gonna Party Like It's 1985

Rekha Kuver

Noah Vickery was the most popular boy in my eighth-grade class. He was blessed by the popularity gods with every trait important to the majority of girls at Dye Junior High. He excelled at baseball, basketball and football, sang in the school choir and got good grades without being perceived as a know-it-all nerd. He had clear skin and straight white teeth that had never experienced the indignity of braces. His deep voice unintentionally mocked other boys who were squeaking their way painfully through puberty. More importantly than all this, Noah had mystique. His quiet brooding reflected an air of mystery and depth. He wore his popularity like a hair shirt: He was undeniably uncomfortable with it but tolerated its inevitability with quiet fortitude. No one could remember a time when Noah wasn't popular. From kindergarten until junior high, Noah walked within a halo of adulation.

I, on the other hand, had popularity thrust upon me. I was the nouveau riche of the popular set, as opposed to Noah's nobility. Not that I had ever been a social outcast at school. I had a lot of friends from many different cliques, but none of the cliques felt overly covetous of me. I floated, quite content, on the periphery.

After the summer of 1985, I entered eighth grade, fully expecting more of the same, when a most astonishing thing occurred. The three most popular girls in school began including me in everything they did. Even now I don't quite know why this happened. I have a sneaking suspicion that it had something to do with the fact that I had attended an out-of-state dance school that summer, which perhaps gave me an aura of sophistication. Still, that explanation didn't occur to me then, and I was overwhelmed with feeling excruciatingly in over my head. Holly, Shelly and Jeannie were willowy and bubbly, with womanly breasts and gigantic hair. They had made out with boys. They had drunk beer and champagne. Their parents hung out at country clubs. They were white, giggled a lot and had flowery handwriting. I was brown, had never even kissed a boy on the cheek, had never taken a drink and had parents who gardened at home for fun. I had all the pulchritude of Olive Oyl from Popeye cartoons. And yet . . .

"Hey, Rekha. You wanna sit with me at lunch today?" That was Holly Budabaugh (leeringly called "Holly Booty-bod" by the boys), leaning over her desk in Mr. May's science class during the filmstrip on cells. With a photo of the process of osmosis silhouetting her sandy blond hair, she smiled and that was that.

That entire year, I felt sucked into a whirlwind. Sitting with Holly and her friends at lunch was only the beginning. I tried out for cheerleading. I made the team (mainly, I think, because I could do the splits) but couldn't be on it because I had dance class after school every day and couldn't make practice. I tried out for a solo in the school choir. We were doing a rendition of "We Are the World," and all the stars' parts would go to different kids, which made for great odds of getting a part. I tried out, nervously thinking I would maybe get a one-line solo that had originally been sung by Daryl Hall or Huey Lewis, but I miraculously got the highly sought-after Michael Jackson chorus. I saw Holly, Shelly and Jeannie every weekend and talked to them endlessly on the phone. I cruised the halls with them between classes and began to think that talking to other kids wasn't that important. Cute boys began to joke around with me and throw innuendo-laden comments my way, most of which I didn't understand. No matter. I was becoming a master of the coy giggle, which covered almost any situation.

And then there was Noah. He began to talk to me in Mrs. Garafolo's English class, and we exchanged crucial information: I helped him diagram sentences and he taught me how to twirl a pencil in one hand like the drummer from Def Leppard. It didn't matter that both talents were equally worthless. At least we were talking. Our conversations remained achingly monosyllabic but increasingly significant.

"You going to the game on Friday?" he would ask, turning his head just enough for me to guess that he was talking to me.

"Yeah."

What more evidence did I need? No one could deny that Noah was interested in me. Aside from the scintillating conversation, he would smile at me in the hall, and Holly and I had even spotted him riding his bike past my house one evening. He didn't live in my neighborhood! This was definitely love.

The school year was coming to an end, and Noah and I weren't getting any closer. What to do? To hurry this affair along, Shelly hatched a scheme that she insisted was genius! We would throw a "boy-girl" party. There had been a boom of such parties given by various kids in our class that year. Boys and girls were invited, Spin the Bottle was played, fast and slow dances were attempted, and punch was consumed. My family's huge basement was the perfect setting for Noah and me finally to proceed to the next phase in our relationship. I was (as usual) nervous about diving into such an archetypal popular-kid activity. I mean, hosting a party at my house? I wasn't sure. But Shelly convinced me. Hadn't they told me I could handle cheerleader tryouts? Hadn't I gotten a great solo after they had urged me to audition? I could hear the unspoken implications: Wasn't I a different person now that these girls had made me one of them?

Almost before I knew what was happening, we had asked my parents for permission, set the date of the shindig, invited the guests and picked out our outfits. I felt severe pangs of guilt when Holly and Jeannie vetoed my desire to invite Melissa Gonzales to the party. Melissa had been my neighbor all through elementary school and had been one of my close friends in my pre-popularity era. Holly and Jeannie wrinkled their cute noses at my suggestion, and so when the first guests' parents pulled into my driveway to drop off their kids the night of the party, I tried not to think about Melissa seeing the arrivals from her bedroom window.

My basement was decorated with twenty dollars' worth of crepe-paper streamers and purple balloons. I had even splurged on red light bulbs for a funky lighting effect, but screwing them in made us all look eerily bloodied, so we took them back out. Shelly and I baked cookies and brownies and placed them on the ping-pong table, next to a large punch bowl full of iced red Kool-Aid with 7 UP added for fizz. My parents remained upstairs after I pleaded with them to stick to their script: "Please. Just answer the door, send the guests downstairs and do *not* come down unless it is an emergency."

Holly, Shelly and Jeannie had come over early to get ready at my house. By the time the guests arrived, I was stunning. By this I don't mean to imply that I looked good. Just stunning. I had poufed my hair out as large as it would go. I didn't have bangs like the other girls, so my hair wasn't really very tall, but it was certainly wide. I sported a pair of black fingerless lace gloves, a red sweatshirt that fell off one shoulder and could easily have held three of me, and jeans with little zippers at the ankles. The two pounds of junk jewelry on my body caused me to jingle like Santa whenever I made the slightest move. I had applied my makeup with the utmost care, making sure that all the colors of the spectrum were democratically represented on my face. Noah would faint dead away when he saw me, I was sure of that.

People arrived energized and ready to get down. Other boy-girl parties usually began with a warm up period, when the boys stood together on one side of the room and the girls on the other. Once the kids had a few cups of stiff Kool-Aid in them, they loosened up and began to dance. Not so at my party. People hit the concrete with their dancing shoes on! Things were going great!

Kevin DeForest and Andy Boyd were shoveling snacks into their mouths with both hands. Margaret Jennings and Sharon Fisher were applying glitter to each other's faces and giggling uncontrollably. Rich Malcolmson was running around with a ruler, measuring the distance between slow dancers like the teachers did at school dances and cracking up to the point of collapse.

I had spotted Noah when he arrived, but now that things

were really swinging I wasn't sure where he had gone. I couldn't turn to any of my pals for help, because all three of them had disappeared into the back room of my basement with three boys and were diligently collecting hickeys on their necks. I walked through the crowd of kids, toward the stairs at the back of the room. Everyone was here. Could he have left already?

I peeked around the corner, up the staircase. There was Noah, dressed in a fresh pair of acid-washed jeans and a crisp peach Ocean Pacific T-shirt. He was sitting in the shadows on the fifth stair up with his friend Brian, his elbows resting lazily against the brown shag carpet. He was looking right at me as my head poked around the corner, as if he was expecting me. Maybe he had heard the telltale jingle of my jewelry. He spoke first.

"Hey."

"Hi."

"How's it going?"

Apparently Brian wasn't going to take part in this conversation.

"Pretty good."

"Good."

This was going *fantastic!*

"What time did you guys get here?" I made a bold move and

sat down on the stair below them. I noticed his Adidas sneakers looked shiny and new, seeming somehow out of place on Noah's feet.

"Eight. I had to shower after basketball practice."

It kind of embarrassed me that he mentioned showering. Then my embarrassment made me feel like a dork. Holly and the rest of them were playing tonsil hockey with boys in the next room, and here I was embarrassed over Noah's hygiene.

"So . . . " He smiled at me as he spoke, so I guessed things were okay.

"Rekha! This punch tastes like shit," shouted someone from the dance floor. I got up.

"Just a sec." Just when things were starting to heat up with Noah! I walked back into the room and went over to the ping-pong buffet. Oh, man. I had set up the punch bowl earlier. I had made a bowl of punch, then put the extra canister of Kool-Aid powder next to the bowl, along with a bag of sugar so that we could make more if we ran low. I looked at the punch bowl now. The five-pound bag of sugar lay empty on the floor, and a syrupy mound of sugar broke through the placid surface of the Kool-Aid.

"Who did this?" I demanded loudly over the sounds of

Madonna singing "Into the Groove." I saw Tommy Schmutzler and Dave Bisbee, two hulking football players with necks the circumference of my thigh, laughing really hard and slapping each other on the back. What to do? Deal with this or go back to the whole point of this party—Noah? Were Holly, Shelly and Jeannie going to kiss and tell, without me?

"Forget it." I left the sugary mess and jingled back over to the stairs. Noah was still there, this time without Brian. Why was he sitting here by himself? Could it be that he was *waiting* for me?

"Hey again," he said, tilting his head to one side. I sat down and smiled brightly, hoping he hadn't seen or heard what had happened in the other room. "Where are all your buddies?"

"Oh, they're around here somewhere." I laughed when this came out of my mouth, and so did he. He knew exactly where they were and what they were doing, which made my stomach feel funny. Was he leading up to something? What if he asked me to go into the back room too? Suddenly I was petrified of this boy.

We sat there silently, not looking at each other. It never occurred to me that he may have been feeling nervous or uncomfortable too. He seemed so impenetrable, so nonchalant.

As I sneaked glances at him, I noticed his tendency to furrow his brow and squint his eyes, as though his thoughts were so deep they pained him.

I thought of asking him to dance, but quickly abandoned that idea. I had never seen Noah dance at other boy-girl parties. I didn't know what to say, and the silence was lengthening. We must have sat there like that for a half-hour or more, not looking at each other or speaking. My mind raced the entire time: *Is this what people do? What is he thinking about? Has he forgotten that I'm here?* I jingled my jewelry a little, just to remind him of my presence. He didn't respond. *This is crazy,* I thought. It was not how I pictured things happening at all. *Maybe he never liked me to begin with?* I yearned for a pencil to twirl or a sentence to diagram.

All of a sudden I noticed something. The party had grown kind of quiet. The laughter and the occasional yelling had stopped. There were still some rumblings of people talking, but compared to earlier, it was practically silent except for the music.

"I'll be right back," I said and got up to head back to the party.

When I went back into the room, all of the kids were standing in clusters along the four walls, like a group of beginning roller skaters afraid to push off into the rink. They were still talking within their groups, but everyone was glancing toward the middle of the dance floor. I couldn't blame them. When I saw what was there, I couldn't stop staring either. Or, more accurately, when I saw *who* was there.

In the middle of my basement, during the middle of my party, like an unbelievable mirage or projected holographic image, were *two high schoolers.* And not just any high schoolers. Jake Castleberry and John Gamble. They were seniors, the kind of seniors whom everyone knew. Jake was the gregarious star of every school musical and John was the achingly gorgeous bagger at the local Thriftway. They were here, in my house, at my party! My immediate thought should have been that this was the most incredible thing that had happened in anyone's recent memory. This was sure to elevate my boy-girl party to the level of legend. Instead, I was terrified.

Jake and John stood there, impossibly real, and ignored the fact that they were at an eighth-grade party. They seemed to be conferring about something and didn't even look my way. Why should they? They'd probably never seen me before. They didn't know it was my party, unless they happened to notice my resemblance to my parents, who let them in.

My parents! Holy smokes, was I in trouble. But they let these guys in. I turned on my heels and did a speed march to the stairs. As I turned to race up them, I practically tripped over Noah.

"Hey! Watch it!" he yelled at me. I had never heard Noah yell, except on the football field or basketball court. He was supposed to be inscrutable, unflappable. And now here he was, yelling at me.

"Sorry." I had bigger things on my mind at the moment. I raced up the stairs, most likely with a look of panic on my made-up rainbow face. Noah got up and followed me.

"What's going on?"

I didn't answer him. I didn't know what awaited me up there. At the top of the stairs, I ran down the hall, my necklaces bouncing off my chest and slapping me in the face, and looked out the front window. There was John's car. The same blue Camaro that he drove to the Thriftway. They had driven here, which meant that my parents had to know they were over sixteen. Crap.

"Whose car is that?" Noah asked me, still following me as I walked toward the living room. I could hear the television, and I wondered how my parents could be watching Balki Bartokomous on *Perfect Strangers* at a time when they should have been plotting my heinous punishment. I rushed into the living room. There sat my parents, calmly watching TV.

"Oh, Rekha, did you see Jeannie's older brother? He's looking for her."

Jeannie?! Neither Jake nor John was related to Jeannie. I tried to cover my confusion.

"Oh. Yeah. Right." I did an about-face and walked back to the stairs. Noah was still walking with me, but at this point I didn't know what was more important: hanging out with Noah or seeing what was happening downstairs.

At the exact moment I had this doubt about Noah's importance, he seemed to sense my attention slipping away from him. He must've thought he had to act fast, because without any warning, he reached over and grabbed my hand.

We seemed to be walking down the hall in slow motion. I thought to myself, *I am holding Noah Vickery's hand. Me and Noah. Holding hands. Touching. Noah is touching me. Noah Vickery. Noah and Rekha.*

I turned my head to smile at Noah. As I completed this maneuver, I glanced out the front window again. I wanted to see the evening's two triumphs in the same moment: Noah smiling at me and John's car in the driveway. Heavenly.

Not so heavenly. The car was gone! I didn't get it. They couldn't have left, not when I didn't really get to bask in the glow of their presence in my house! Plus, Noah hadn't seen them here! Holly, Shelly and Jeannie probably hadn't either!

When we got back downstairs, the scene had changed again. There was some kind of commotion going on. Noah dropped my hand and stared at Jake and John, who were not only still there, but were charging toward me with Jeannie in tow. Jeannie had Rich Malcolmson's ruler and gesticulated with it as she spoke.

"Rekha, we kind of have a problem," she said, smiling at me wanly. "Umm, Jake and John are here because they want to find out where my sister is. You know, my sister was dating Jake." I stood there dumbly. Noah had disappeared, and I was being cornered into having to talk in front of Jake and John. Jeannie continued, "Well, Jake went to my house looking for my sister, and my mom told him that she was picking me up here at ten o'clock. But really, I'm getting a ride with Shelly's folks, so my sister isn't coming here."

What did all this mean? Why was she telling me all this useless information? Why was everyone staring at me? I had the feeling I was supposed to say something. Jake and John were looking at me like I had done something terrible and they were waiting for me to explain myself. I looked helplessly at Jeannie.

"Well, umm, when they got here, they put their car keys on the ping-pong table. Now the keys are gone."

I couldn't believe this. Just when things were going so well, now Jeannie was telling me someone *stole* a car? Someone in our class was capable of grand theft auto?

"The thing is, Tommy Schmutzler thought it would be funny to take the car for a spin. He took Holly with him." She turned to Jake and John. "They're just kidding around. They should be back any minute."

Jake and John continued to glare at me. Jeannie handed me the ruler as if she was passing me the baton of responsibility for this whole situation and simply walked away, the heart-shaped hickeys on her neck blazing like proud combat scars.

Twenty minutes later, the party had broken up. My parents were so proud of the quietness of the party, the apparent lack of mischief and the maturity of my friends that they had gone to bed and let me handle the goodbyes and thank-yous. By ten o'clock, everyone had gone, all of them telling me that this was the most awesome party they had ever been to—everyone, that is, except for Jake and John. John's car had yet to turn up. The two sat in angry silence on my front porch, peering down the street in hopes of seeing some headlights. They hadn't spoken a word to me and somehow seemed to blame me for what had happened to the car. I lay in the grass in the front yard, the stupid ruler across my stomach, exhausted and alone. I didn't realize anyone else was still there until I saw someone sitting on the grass beside me. It was Noah. For the first time ever, I initiated the conversation.

"What are you still doing here?" I was tired and I felt miserable. Shelly and Jeannie had left without offering to help me clean up, and they had seemed uninterested in me with the same suddenness with which they had become interested in me last fall. I had begun to suspect that this entire party had been some sort of final trial that they had put me through. Throwing a boy-girl party was actually a popularity litmus test. Making out, remaining serene, maintaining some sense of bravado were the hoops I was supposed to hurdle through. I hadn't done any of these things. My panic throughout the evening had been ridiculously evident to them, I was sure. And now here I was with Noah, and I was so worn out by this time that a coy giggle never even entered my mind.

"I told my mom to pick me up at ten-thirty by accident."

"Oh." What would have seemed like a preordained miracle

of destiny an hour ago now did nothing for me. I rubbed my sleepy eyes with the back of my hand and noticed the mottled mixture of eye shadow smeared across my knuckles.

"That party was really great."

At that moment, two things became official. One, Noah was finally trying to impress me with a compliment. Two, I finally didn't care. Sitting there in the soggy grass, my exhaustion had started to sprout small drops of clarity.

"Thanks." I felt like I wanted to say something more to Noah. Something real. I wanted to ask him how he could deal with all this popularity stuff, ask him if it tired him out on a daily basis the way I was worn-out now. Ask him if he was interested in me because I was friends with the popular girls or for some other more substantial reason. Ask him about his family, or what he really liked so much about sports, or tell him that I really hated Def Leppard even though I did think the drumstick twirl was impressive. I didn't know where to begin with all the things I suddenly wanted to say to him.

"There they are!" Noah pointed down the street. A car was driving toward my house at about three miles an hour with the headlights off. I sat up. Jake and John stood up. The car crept along, painfully slow. I could make out the corpulent head that undoubtedly belonged to Tommy Schmutzler in the driver's seat. He was gripping the steering wheel and gazing intently at the road in front of him. He was leaning forward, with his chest flat against the steering wheel, and it was apparent that the car was in neutral and simply coasting along. Holly was in the back seat, her four-inch vertical blond bangs reflecting the moonlight. As they inched closer, Holly waved at all of us cheerily as though she were on a float in a parade.

Jake and John ran down the driveway. Tommy managed to stop the car, and he slid over into the passenger seat. John got in and shoved Tommy a little, yelling that he was a dumbfuck and that he was lucky nothing had happened to his car. Jake got in the back with Holly and they all sped off together. Apparently John was angry enough to keep yelling at Tommy but not quite angry enough to kick him out of the car.

Noah and I sat alone, but before I could think of what would happen next, another car turned the corner and began to drive toward us.

"Well, I might as well meet my mom at the end of the driveway." Noah seemed to be hesitating. Maybe he wanted to say something real to me too. Maybe he sensed that I was no longer supremely jazzed about everything he did. Maybe he had started to see, now that I could finally bring myself to look him in the eyes, that popularity inspired in me only pressure and utter fatigue, not excitement for my friends or flegdling desire for him. Maybe he was exactly the same as he always was, but I was just seeing him differently now.

"Okay." I smiled at him and knew that this was the last hurrah of the Popular Rekha Era. I would probably still be friends with Holly, Jeannie, Shelly and Noah, but not in the same way as I had been all year. I began to understand that I could know them on *my* terms; I didn't have to be a part of their game simply because they had picked me.

We stood up and brushed the grass off our jeans. I tried to think of where to begin to tell him some part of what I was feeling, when Noah grabbed me by the shoulders, pulled me toward him and clobbered my face in a head-on collision kiss. Before I could think about what was happening, he turned around and ran toward the street, not pausing to look back or wave before getting into his mom's car.

I rubbed my face where my teeth ached from the smooch

attack. I looked over toward Melissa Gonzales's house. All the lights were off. I knew I wasn't going to tell Holly, Shelly or Jeannie about what had just happened. I thought of telling Melissa though. I turned toward my house and walked to the front door, twirling my ruler like a drumstick, grateful to be heading back toward the periphery.

A Clean Break

Allison Fraiberg

I knew I was a goner when I saw her effortlessly open a second can of diet soda while she sucked the last gulp of the first can then dropped it into the recycling bin. It was one smooth motion, a choreographed ballet of commercial sensibility. This was a woman who could chain-drink soda. No shame, no apology, just a matter-of-fact ability to determine her own limits, her own serving size.

It's pretty easy to see how I could fall for a woman like that. After all, I had just spent six years with a woman who didn't even like soda—her politics forbade it. Only when all other resources were exhausted would she take a sip, accepting it from my hand in much the same way a wary child might approach a stranger. As the postindustrial poison infiltrated her mouth and throat, horrible sounds of suffering would escape her being. For her, a sip of soda necessitated a Newtonian reaction that sounded like a wretched human hairball. It shouldn't have bothered me that much, I know. After all, we had done great things together. We had protested the Gulf War, rallied support to sustain legal abortion and collaborated with our community to raise awareness about AIDS. We were educators, social activists determined to make a difference.

But was it so wrong to want a "regular girl"? To let loose and watch cheesy sit-coms, listen to music with shallow lyrics and devour the fine print of *Entertainment Weekly?* I admit it, I wanted someone who wasn't shy about living vibrantly within popular culture, someone who didn't demand an adversarial relationship to everything mainstream. Since when had fighting for social justice and just plain socializing become mutually exclusive endeavors? To find someone who happily drank that cancer-causing, corporate-manufactured diet soda made me believe I could have that regular girl I dreamed of.

With the sudden *splooosh* of an opening can, she made the regular world overflow and teem with bubbles.

So, you see, I was a goner by the time that commercial-perfect soda-drinking incident occurred. We had known each other for a few weeks by then. We'd been to concerts together almost every night, watched a stream of trashy videos and consumed mounds of processed sugar. We were well on our way to falling in love. Finally, I had found my relationship with a regular girl. The sad part, of course, was that she lived in the Northwest and I lived in Southern California. We were separated. But that only made for a more romantic courtship. She would send me CDs and I would tell her my stories of celebrity sightings. We emailed obsessively all hours of the day and night. We ran up huge phone bills, often missing meetings or classes because we couldn't bear to say goodbye. Finally, she came to visit me in L.A.

She got off the plane with a duffle bag in one hand, a slick electric guitar in the other and a smile that shot across the gate area and settled in my heart. The guitar and smile were for me, one to feed my rock-star delusions and the other to feed my aching soul. We hugged, long and firm, with our bodies touching from neck to toe. Still feeling the thrill of the hug all over us, we turned to leave the airport to start what was going to be the most romantic weekend of our lives.

Shortly after we got to my place, she slammed a can of soda. I didn't have the words to tell her why her drinking a second soda was igniting such passion within me, so I didn't say a word and instead stopped what I was doing and took her in my arms. We spent the rest of the evening making love. It wasn't tender, goofy lovemaking either; this was wild, rolling, romping sex during which we flopped, slopped and wrestled our way from one rippling orgasm to the next. I never did tell her about how her soda thirst provoked my own sexual thirst. I do know that throughout the evening we inhaled a good deal more of that soda, an act that both quenched and compelled anew my desire for her.

At some point, we managed to get out of bed and do things that weekend. Our adventures took us to the ocean, and we walked along the Santa Monica pier. It was January, but warm enough to enjoy the kisses of sea salt in the air. The flirting ocean seduced us back to childhood, so we found ourselves playing air hockey in a pier arcade and feeding each other ice cream and hot pretzels. We finished the afternoon over at

McCabe's Guitar Shop, strumming guitars and fantasizing about our favorite musicians who had played there.

It was one of those days that, if it were in a film, would be captured in a slow-motion montage with fabulously romantic background music. We finally returned to my house around five to shower and change for dinner. She jumped in the shower first and I picked up my place a bit from the night before. I emulated her toss as I threw the empty soda cans into the recycling bin. I picked up some candy wrappers, some socks and a couple of T-shirts. Then I made the bed because I wanted the erotic charge of ripping it all apart again that night when we got home. And after dinner, we did just that.

The next day, our adventures took us up to the historically decadent Hollywood sign. We drove up and down Mulholland and Laurel Canyon, trying to spot celebrities driving home, but only ended up seeing Ed Begley, Jr., riding his bike through the hills, which doesn't even count. Once again, we swaggered home, but this time we never did make it back out to dinner. Later, at that critical moment when after-sex dozing can turn quickly into hard night's sleep, I shook myself awake to go wash up. We had fallen asleep naked and when I moved, it seemed as though our skin had melted together. I felt her completely, and pulling away, our skin separated slowly and deliberately. As I got out of bed, I couldn't help but run my hand along the arm that had been under her as if I could still feel her skin pressed to mine. Lost in the reverie, I tripped over what I thought must have been a disgruntled cat displaced from his usual spot on the bed. When no howl or hiss emerged, however, I realized he wasn't the culprit; it was her jeans. Of course, I realized, we had undressed each other as we made our way to bed earlier. When I hit three more piles of her belongings before reaching my bedroom door, I had to laugh. *Silly messy girl,* I thought as I gathered the mini-piles into one substantial mound. I turned the dimmer light on slightly in the bathroom and reached for my toothpaste. She had put some of her toiletries on the counter, and her brush and hair mousse had slipped into the sink. I gathered all the items into a neat corner of the counter and remembered how we were in a rush this morning, so it's no wonder some stuff ended up out of place. I finished washing up and went back to bed to feel our skin become one again.

In the morning, she had to return home. A final semester of law school awaited her, and I had to get ready for a new semester at the campus where I taught. We lingered in bed as long as we could, wrapped in each other and taking turns giving the cats some much needed attention. Glancing around the room, looking for a cat toy of some sort, I couldn't help but notice the new heaps of shorts, pants and shirts that had accumulated. Even some workout gear hung drying on the electric guitar, which I had displayed on a shiny new stand purchased at McCabe's. I had no idea how the clothes had gotten there. I had just tidied up last night, and I could have sworn that she hadn't hauled herself out of bed for more than five minutes. She went through clothes much like she polished off soda: wildly and quickly. And she left piles of both around.

I shrugged; we had to pack anyway and this was our last day together. She stuffed everything in the duffle bag about ten minutes before we left for the airport. Holding hands in the car, we looked longingly at each other when we hit traffic lights, dreading the inevitable departure. We didn't talk through the check-in process or on the walk to the gate; we were in each other's thoughts and sound seemed intrusive. When the flight attendant nodded to us and announced the final call to board, we stood up to say goodbye. We hugged, not long but penetrating and close enough to whisper, "I love you," to each other.

I walked back to the car, my face red from both tears and a torrent of emotion that bled all over me. The drive home seemed long and I could feel again the ominous and quiet desperation that sits over this city. For a few days, she had held the city at bay for me. The cats greeted me at the door with forgiving meows that echoed in the now-empty hallway. I missed her already. I began cleaning up the place and let my mind replay the brilliant red blistery memories of the weekend.

We slipped back into our routine of long phone calls and multiple daily emails. But she hadn't really left, in a way, at least not all of her. Two weeks went by and I found myself still discovering little remnants of her visit—a bandanna behind the bed, two half-eaten boxes of Hot Tamales in the bedside drawer, some socks on the floor of the closet. I began to wonder about my love's habits.

She eased my fears, however, when during a particularly lusty email she let me know that she was cleaning her house like a fiend. She had never found herself so inspired to embark on such a project, but somehow being with me had energized her. She was gutting the place, she said, sorting though piles of old papers, mountains of forgotten clothes, even braving the depths of her basement. Her breaks from studying the intricacies of constitutional law consisted alternately of digging into a new house-cleaning project and calling me to report on her progress. It was a splendid time—silly, fun, productive. And my worries about a piggish partner subsided.

By February, we had planned and booked my first visit to her home. I was giddy with excitement, I couldn't wait to see her again, and I'll admit I was thrilled at the prospect of seeing all she had done with her house. The plane seemed to take forever and the biting, damp cold of the winter air in the Northwest knocked the Southern California wind out of me when the automatic doors at the airport thrust us out into the open parking lot. She was bravely sweet in her attempts to protect me from the invasive cold, trying to block the wind, hurrying our pace to the car and shuffling me into the passenger seat. With my bag in the trunk and the car engine doing its best to warm the stiff vinyl seats, she blew her hands warm and wrapped me up in her embrace. We chatted about everything and nothing; it didn't matter because we were together again. When she pulled the car into her driveway, I got my first peek at the sturdy brick house. The exterior was cute, but nothing out of the ordinary, which was fine, because the real excitement lay inside: What had she created for us in her home? What had come of these weeks of cleaning? This moment would obliterate all of the ridiculous doubts festering at the back of my mind.

The front door opened into the living room and kitchen. I took one step in past the tiny foyer and didn't even hear her shut the heavy wood door behind us. I wasn't surprised that I could smell the dogs right away. This, this was the cleaned version of the house? This was the result of days and days of tortured purging, gutting and dismantling? I shuddered when I imagined what it must have looked like before.

Before I could turn around and run back to the airport, she asked in a voice begging for validation, "Well, what do you think?" I don't remember much of the next few hours, only that something came out of my mouth to answer her question and it must have placated her in some way because I was still there the next day. Maybe it was her pleading blue eyes, or maybe it was her hand holding mine in a way that could both completely protect me and convey her own vulnerability, but I stayed and I swear she never knew what I thought about her officially piggy ways.

At the end of the week, she took me back to the airport, and in the clean, swept halls of the concourse all I could think about was how good it felt to hold her, to see the blush of her cheek when she looked at me. Outside that house, she was the girl of my dreams and when I crumbled into the rough seat of the plane, all I could feel was the emptiness of the window seat beside me. Back in Los Angeles, the images of the house faded each time I took out the photos that captured our time together. I looked at them constantly, each glance evoking the scent of perfumed desire, the touch of cool silky skin and the taste of a salty goodbye tear.

I longed for her. As springtime passed, the miles became harder to bear and her graduation from law school approached swiftly. She was ready to start a new life and ached to spend it with me in L.A. Her years in law school had clearly paid off because she had convinced me to move in with her. She was going to move her whole life down here for me; couldn't I at least move across town for her? I guess so. By May, she had moved to Los Angeles and we had a rented a small house in a part of town near several movie and television studios. I think I said yes because I believed that this new house would be different, it would be *our* house, something that we would create together, something that would be influenced by both of our characters. Yes, this house would be different.

I still remember talking on the phone with her mother one day a few weeks after we had moved in. She asked me how I felt about her daughter's—what did she call it—"household habits," and I remember her incredulous giggle when I told her that this was our house and things would be different here. When I heard the other extension pick up, I said goodbye, and I could hear the closed-mouth chuckle fade off as I hung up the phone. Her mother was right, of course, and this house would be no different than anywhere else she had lived.

Life went on though and I created spaces for her and spaces for me. The living room and my office were near the front of the house, and I had control over them. There were hardwood floors and some luscious woodwork in the house, so I focused on that and created a decent living space. When service people came to the house, I made sure to keep them in my area or tried to be at work during scheduled appointments. I met neighbors at their homes and insisted on meeting my friends out for dinner. It really wasn't that hard to work around. She was Oscar to my Felix and, no matter what, the world melted away whenever she looked at me.

One afternoon the following spring, I was moving through the house with a broom and dustpan scraping up scattered dog bones and kibble. Earlier that day, I had bagged up another bin full of soda cans, the romantic luster of which had worn off months ago. I had just been working in the bathroom to clear the floor and counter of leaves, sand, weeds, cotton balls, stray hairs and various other forms of wildlife—all hidden under pounds and pounds of clothes. She came up behind me, stood on a pile of clean clothes and asked if we could talk about something important. Her eyes looked sad and anxious; whatever this was about was something that had clearly been troubling her for a while. We sat down on the bed and I put a clean sheet over the crumpled stained blanket she had been using. She sighed as she saw me do this and took my hand. "I can't do this anymore," she said. "I've tried and I've tried and you know I love you. I love you so much."

I could see her mouth moving, but I couldn't connect the

words. If she loved me, then what couldn't she do anymore? I didn't have to wait long for an answer. "What is it?" I pleaded with her.

"I tried to put it out of my mind in the beginning because I was just so crazy about you, and then when I moved down here I thought getting this house together would be different, that it could work."

I could hear the words now, but nothing had prepared me for her next revelation.

"I can't do it," she confessed, taking a gulp of her Diet Dr Pepper. "I can't live with an absolute neat-freak. You're just over the edge with this; you're not normal. It's over, I'm sorry."

Sugar-Coated Breakup

Lori Oliva

It was the kind of Saturday morning that made even the earliest riser want to stay in bed all day. From my half-comatose state, I could hear shriveled leaves blowing past my door, scratching their way down the sidewalk. It was miserable outside, and knowing that I could sleep in during a blustery early morning was very comforting. I was home in my cozy bed, after a grueling week of business travel. A week of delayed flights, budget hotel rooms, cranky clients and bad food made me relish the fact that I was exactly where I wanted to be: at home, safe and sound.

I had missed Jim. I always missed him when I was away for

longer than a day. Many times the only things that kept me going were knowing that I'd see him again soon and wondering about the unusual way that he'd welcome me home. Most often he expressed his affection with the latest bike accessory. From an alligator horn to a chili pepper seat, my bike took on a different look with every business trip that called me away. I had never met anyone quite like him. Quick with a humorous rhyme or clever anecdote, every conversation held the promise of a good laugh. With several distinctive physical characteristics, he was a living anachronism. A stocky build atop his five-foot-ten structure accentuated his girth and contradicted his active lifestyle. It was poetic.

He owned the coolest bike shop in town, which seemed to give him license to be as offbeat as he wanted. The thought of being trapped behind a desk on a sun-crisped day sent him pedaling to the hills in search of unexplored territory. The shop's atmosphere was infectious. On any given day pro racers, tattooed messengers and wide-eyed novices could be found discussing the latest cycling trends under rows of suspended high-end mountain bikes hanging from the ceiling like hens in a French market.

Many days I'd make up excuses to get out of the office for an extended lunch just so I could watch him in action. I'd always try to bring him something to eat: a sandwich, soup, *plat du jour* from the gourmet take-out down the street. But the only thing that really seemed to interest him was the daily bakery special, which might include a signature cookie, depending on who was working the counter.

Without fail, his eyes always lit up when he saw me, sending a surge of adrenaline through my body. "What do you have for me today?" he'd ask coyly. The logo across the wax-coated paper bag gave it away, but I played along. "Chicken salad from Alessi's," I'd say extending the bag. "With a little something extra."

He'd grab the bag, hold up the small morsel and, like a chameleon snatching an unsuspecting fly, pop the sugarcoated nugget into his mouth, licking the residue in quiet satisfaction. It started the same way every time. I'd cautiously extend the bag, prepared to release it quickly; he'd rifle through it, take out the sandwich and turn it over, holding the corner between his two fingers, and catch the powdery treat in the palm of his hand. Sometimes he'd let it sit there while the warmth of his body melted the sugar, giving him reason to run his tongue up the center of his hand like a child finishing a Pixi-Stik.

The first clue that something wasn't quite right was when I discovered that he began to expect the miniature dessert.

"Where's my cookie? I can't eat my sandwich without the little cookie!" The ranting went on until I agreed to go back.

Yes, it was strange behavior, but everyone has hang-ups. I try to be forgiving because I'm not without my own. For example, I can't walk into a public place without shoes. Many people can just hop out of their cars and run into a 7-Eleven barefoot. I can't. The mere thought of shuffling across dirty linoleum makes my skin crawl. A gritty floor underfoot combined with parking lot grease, cookie crumbs, Dip Stix mix, sticky Slurpee juice and God knows what else makes me want to take a Silkwood shower.

Back to the morning after I returned from Denver. With low temperatures and gray skies, staying in my tight cocoon of fresh cotton sheets and a snug goose down comforter was the only thing I craved. As a toast-and-coffee girl, I usually had breakfast without ever having to step outside. But I suspected that if Jim didn't get his sugar fix before 10 A.M., there'd be trouble.

I tried to ignore his incessant poking, but after the fourth prod at my rib I finally gave in. I pulled the covers from over my head to see his face looming at me. "Good morning, sleepy-head," he said with boyish enthusiasm.

His devilish grin made me forget any selfish desire to hibernate. "Joe! Joe! Joe! Joe!" he chanted. My homemade coffee didn't do it for him. He needed professional brew and before I knew it, I was sitting in the passenger seat, watching him drive past the eclectic eateries that dotted my midtown neighborhood.

The sun, just starting to break through the overbearing clouds, gave off just enough glare to make me wish I had worn sunglasses. As I pulled down the visor, I noticed the quick flash of cars passing with early risers getting a jump-start on their weekend. Focused on completing the errands of the day, the drivers all seemed to have the same blank gaze. It made me wonder where they were going and why they were so intent on getting there. It was then that I was startled out of my precaffeinated daze by a loud bellow. "That's it!" he yelled, lifting his hand from the steering wheel. "Oh," he giggled. "And the sign's lit."

"That's what?" I gasped.

He pointed to the towering white steel monolith emblazoned with red neon, and smirked. Seemingly engaged in an internal battle, he debated whether he should let me in on the sixty-plus-year-old secret that all Krispy Kreme disciples know. "You don't know?" he asked mockingly. "When the red Hot Doughnuts Now sign lights up, the doughnuts are fresh out of the fryer!"

I hoped that my silence was evidence that I wasn't impressed.

He cocked his head in amazement. "You mean to tell me that you've never had a hot Krispy Kreme doughnut?"

He seemed genuinely alarmed by my answer.

"Well, get ready to be introduced to a whole new world of doughnut delicacy," he said as he caressed the back of my head, his manner a weird mix of condescension and deep love.

His gesture made me feel shy; my eyes drifted down toward the floorboard. It was then that I saw his toes tapping to the beat of music and his bare foot on the brake pedal.

It was one thing to demand that we attempt this seemingly ridiculous venture first thing in the morning, but it was quite another to do it barefoot. "You don't have on any shoes!" I wailed. "You can't go in there without any shoes!" I cursed myself for not noticing his lack of footwear before we left the house, but he was in the car before I even had a chance to brush my teeth.

"I'll just be in there for a minute." His patience with me was waning.

"No!" I shrieked. "You could cut yourself on a broken beer bottle or soda tab or something."

He squinted his eyes in scrutiny. "Uh, they don't make soda tabs anymore."

I tried to convince him that there could be a lit cigarette under his naked foot. He looked at me as if he wasn't sure if he should respond. "Listen, they're not going to enforce the no-shoes, no-service rule for a couple of doughnuts."

Immediate relief washed over me as we pulled up to the drive-thru and a deadpan voice greeted us over the intercom.

"Welcome to Krispy Kreme."

Without hesitating, Jim barked out the order. "Six . . . no, twelve—yeah, a dozen—glazed and two large coffees, please."

He turned to me. "Are you happy?" he asked. "We don't even have to get out of the car."

We pulled up to the second window and an arm attached to a faceless body held out a white box adorned with green dots and red cursive lettering. He grabbed it, ripped it open and quickly sank his teeth into the yeasty confection.

One bite led to another then another. "Yummmm!" It was the only sound he could make without spitting frosting all over the front seat. In five bites the round, sticky mass was gone, leaving only traces of milky sugar glaze at the corners of Jim's mouth. His orgasmic expression sickened me as I watched his eyes roll back in his head, and like an addict with a fresh fix, he sat fulfilled in the glory of the moment.

I could feel the bile churning in the pit of my stomach. I could only turn my head in disgust.

"You'd better hurry up!" he said as he reached for another. "These beauties are getting colder by the second!" He stuffed half a doughnut in his mouth and tossed the box onto my lap.

From the second it hit my thighs I could feel heat radiating from it. I lifted the mangled lid and removed one of the doughnuts from its nest of discarded glaze and took a bite. I have to admit that it did offer a certain sensual pleasure. It was as though I had bitten into a soft, warm cloud, like cotton candy on a hot summer day. It dissolved in my mouth almost as fast as I bit into it.

But even the sinful goodness of a hot Krispy Kreme doughnut couldn't make up for my disgust at Jim's overzealous sweet tooth. My heart pumped inside my chest as I struggled to stay calm while thinking of how to get out of this nightmare.

I thought I'd give him a chance to repent, to redeem himself, to show that he had some self-control. "Let's get some exercise today. Maybe a bike ride?" I suggested. *Say something! Anything!*

I screamed to myself as he sat silently licking his lips. I hated him more the longer he contemplated the thought.

"On a full stomach?"

That's not an answer! I thought as I watched him eye the box. He grabbed another doughnut and jammed it into his mouth. By that point, he wasn't even chewing. He consumed one bite after another, swallowing as fast as he could to make room for the next mouthful.

It was then that something came over me. To this day, I still cannot quite figure out what triggered it. Maybe it was my own sugar high. Maybe it was the realization that if I let this relationship continue, I'd be the one with the problem. But somewhere in between bites of that heavenly, cottony, fried dough, I lost it.

"I can't take it anymore!" I screamed as I slammed my fist on the dashboard.

"What?" he yelled, shocked at my outburst.

"This," I said, opening my arms in a gesture that put our relationship in the middle of a two-foot space between the palms of my hands. "The doughnuts, the bingeing, the obsession of where your next sugar fix is coming from. I can't take it!"

"You're being silly. Have another doughnut." He looked at me with expressionless, black eyes. I knew whatever I said would evoke the same placid response. His denial drove me further into my rage.

"You've got a sweet tooth on steroids and it's driving me crazy!"

His stomach bumped the steering wheel as he took a deep breath and resettled in the seat. He was restless but silent, and I wanted to ask if he was okay but couldn't. I couldn't say anything. He sighed and wiped his lips with the thin, paper napkin, sending crusted glaze falling to his chest.

"Do you know what it's like," he asked, "to crave satisfaction?"

The question dumbfounded me. Satisfaction? I realized then that it was a much deeper issue. "Satisfaction can't be delivered in a doughnut or a cookie," I said.

"Yes, it can," he chuckled. "So I have a sweet tooth, so what? What about you? Ms. Paranoid to Step Outside Without Shoes. You've got some hang-ups there yourself."

Oh, that's rich, I thought, but this burning issue didn't need any more fuel. I think that it was the first time that I used the training from my psychology minor. All of the classes came rushing back to me, making me face the ugly realization that dependency issues and diffused blame go hand in hand. What

I didn't realize is that the tables turn very quickly when you're dealing with someone who doesn't think they have a problem.

Yes, I had unresolved issues of my own, but at least I knew the difference between a human friend and a confectionary one. I also knew that there was no reasoning with an addict. He didn't need a girlfriend—he needed a pastry chef.

"I'm sorry," I said as I reached for his arm. "I know that I'm not perfect, but I just can't stand to watch you eat the way you do. I don't think it's healthy."

"Well, I don't think it should concern you so much." He reached for another doughnut to punctuate the statement.

He was right: It shouldn't concern me, and at that moment, I let it go. Immediately, I felt light, as if an anvil had been lifted from my chest. Control, I realized, is almost as toxic as denial.

When we first started dating, I talked myself into overlooking this one bad trait. Blinded by the newness of it all, I told myself that I could change him, although deep down, I knew better.

He continued driving, offering only an occasional curse when caught at a traffic light. The silence told me that he wanted to get home as badly as I did.

He pulled up to my apartment, took the doughnuts and walked me to my door.

"I'm the one who's sorry," he said as he kissed me goodbye. "I love sweets. So what? It's not as if I'm a serial killer. The fact that it bothers you so much tells me that you're not the right woman for me."

Mixed emotions brewed in the pit of my stomach. The selfish side of me didn't want it to be over, but the rational side knew that it was the best thing for both of us. Oh, sure, we may have an occasional coffee or share opinions on the best wheel fork or bike frame, but knowing that I would never have to watch another crumb fall from his mouth gave me newfound freedom and strength.

"You're right," I said with a half-smile. "I wish things could be different." He stood looking at me, waiting for me to clarify myself, as if an explanation of my outburst could somehow salvage the relationship. No words came to mind.

"Is that it?" His eyes grew wider as he anticipated my answer.

"I guess so."

I knew at this point in time that he wasn't about to give up his compulsive behavior for me or anyone else. Maybe one day he'd find his confectionary soul mate—someone who can keep up with him bite after bite. I watched him walk down the corridor with the tattered doughnut box under his arm and wished him well. The only thing I could do was smile and say, "Goodbye."

I keep a photo of Jim on my refrigerator, and I look at it often. It's from our first trip together, at a romantic beach dinner in front of a golden sunset. A captured moment of carefree times, basking in happiness with wine glasses in hand and relaxed smiles on our faces—me in my tennis shoes and him with his key lime pie.

The Home Wrecker

Jennifer Hacock

Let's get married," I'd say to him. After three years of living together, this conversation would come up while we were doing the dishes or driving the car or watching the hockey game.

"No," he'd answer bluntly, without taking his eyes off the water or the road or the television screen.

Oh, he'll come around, I thought. *He just needs time. Give him time.*

I figured he simply needed his own space to see how special we were together, how great he had it with me, how wonderful a gal I was! He'd certainly see it, if I just gave him time.

Meanwhile, in that time, there was his family to get to know better, and I set straight to work. His father and I talked about local and federal politics, World War II history and whether or not Isaac Albéniz piano solos were "Spanish enough." His brother and sister, four years and six years older respectively, greeted me warmly at every family gathering. I became friends with their spouses and felt at home in their exclusive in-law club, despite the fact that my ring finger never got a funny tan line in the summer. Later, I would celebrate with the family at the birth of their six grandchildren, all of whom over the course of eight and a half years considered me "Aunt Jen." But, try as I might, I couldn't figure out his mother with the same ease. At first, I weighed the pros: She was from a small farming community and so was I. She could make pies from scratch and I could bake my grandmother's chocolate chip cookies without looking at the recipe. These were valid similarities. Sure, we may have been forty years apart, but on some deep wild-woman level, we were two peas in a pod. Oh, she just needed time to warm up to me.

"Let's get married," I'd ask him. Same question. Different day. Another year gone.

"I'm not ready," he'd reply, turning away from me as fast as he could.

"When *will* you be ready?" I'd ask, following him around our apartment like a puppy needing a walk. All I wanted was a time frame. I'd wait for my chance at planning a future, a wedding, a honeymoon, a baby, but for how long? A month? Ten years? Anything. I wanted him to throw me a bone.

"I don't know," he would sigh, a sure sign of how tired he was to hear me talk about this. Again.

I kept convincing myself that it was fine. I was fine with not tying this elusive knot. *Who needs a blessing from God anyway? I kept thinking. I don't need Him meddling in my life too. I'm better off this way. I'll just stay calm and sit patiently. My mother always said that good things come to those who wait.*

His sister was getting married though, something his mother seemed eternally relieved about, and I was delighted to have been asked to sing at the church service. It raised my confidence about how entwined I was in his family. I received a present from her, a thank-you for my involvement. The black velvet box held a gold bracelet with matching earrings.

"Oh my." I hadn't expected anything. Nice.

"Thank you very much," I said.

But the matriarch was there, sipping a cup of tea with a pointed pinkie.

"There was a necklace to go with them," she said, vacuuming the wind out of my sails as thoroughly as she did her Chinese carpets. "But it was too expensive."

I see.

"We don't need to get married, Jen. We're good like this," he'd say. "Right?" Same topic. Different day. Yet another year over.

Sure. Fine. I'm great with that. Yessirree! And although I agreed to his face, I'd often have to turn around and stifle the nausea that accompanied the crush in my chest cavity. No wedding yet. No plans for babies. No real reason to practice my calligraphy for dainty shower invitations.

He had an old girlfriend who seemed to be the apple of his mother's eye because this girl had started a family of her own, had had babies and seemed to be a happy healthy housewife—in other words, everything that I was not. His mother used to talk about her in front of me, usually while I was eating.

"I got *another* letter from *Leah* the other day."

"*Leah* is doing really well. You should see pictures of her youngest son."

"Look at the birthday card I got from *Leah*. It would be nice if you gave her a call sometime. She still asks about you."

Jennifer Hacock

I had a limited appetite when she spoke about *Leah*. I started dropping my name in conversation just so she wouldn't forget what it was. This may have come as a shock to her, but *Leah* was certainly in the past. However, like the Jason character that simply cannot be killed off, his mother had a way of reviving *Leah* in her son's life, in our life, the zombie that keeps following you even when you think you've outrun it.

Ring, ring. I answered it.

"Hello?"

"Hi. I'm just calling to see how you guys are," his mother oozed.

"Oh, we're fine. How are the grandkids?"

"Oh, they're good. You should have seen what Emma did the other day. Oh, it was sooo funny."

I stayed, anticipating a cute-because-I-love-her story about Emma, when I heard her turn slightly away from the mouthpiece to ask her husband a question.

"Gerry?" she muffled. "What was that thing that Emma was holding the other day? I'm on the phone to *Leah*."

Even today I wonder why I felt it was inappropriate to tell her of her mistake. Frankly, she scared me. She called me Leah three times before she started listening to herself.

"Have I been calling you *Leah* all this time?" she asked, not extremely horrified.

Well, yes, yes, you have but that's fine. I know what you meant to say . . .

"Ha! Gerry! I've been calling her *Leah* all this time!" She cackled, and followed it closely with belly laughter. But her laugh was directed *at me*. I started having nightmares. Nightmares about toothless old hags beating me with vacuum hoses and duster rags. I started breaking out in embarrassing armpit sweats on the drive over to her house. I tried to think of everything, anything to converse with her about, things she would find interesting: baking, shopping, her grandkids. I'd sit in her kitchen feigning interest and amazement at 101 different scone recipes. I read her town newspaper, catching up on local goings-on and flipped through her Ikea catalogues.

"So, what do you think about the council approving the removal of the trees in the park in order to pave a parking lot?" I would ask her.

"Oh, wow! Look at the price of this duvet cover. And there are sheets to match!"

"Did you know that chickpeas are on sale at Dominion? I'll have to make my hummus for you sometime."

I tried everything, but my feigned fascination with the dull trappings of her life wore me down after a while. I told my boyfriend about my fears. I felt like I needed some comfort.

"You're crazy," he snapped, sloughing me off like dead skin on a loofah.

"No!" I pleaded. "I'm not. I don't think she likes me."

"Don't be daft. Of course she likes you. You know how she is."

Right, I thought. *I'm sure I'm just being silly and paranoid and super sensitive and premenstrual.*

She was no axe wielder, after all.

So she called me by someone else's name? She still had a relationship with that Leah woman. I couldn't take that away from her. It's not like she called me Leah *all* the time. Right? So the necklace was expensive. That's okay because I probably wouldn't have worn it anyway. Too much jewelry makes me look fat.

He was right, as usual.

I started sleeping through the night again. I didn't sweat stains that ran the length of my arms. I was my own woman. I was a great person. I was sure she saw my confidence. All of the grinning and bearing was really paying off!

• • •

Yet another year went by and with it another Christmas season arrived bringing new hope, renewed faith and maybe, just maybe, a small (ring-sized?) blue box for me under the tree. Although we were spending the holidays with his family, I was looking forward to it anyway. Funny, the troubles that rum and eggnog can cover up. This year there was to be a family picture taken by a professional photographer. I got ready for it like everybody else. I poofed up my fine hair for the occasion, dressed in a flattering shade of emerald and occupied a well-deserved seat between my boyfriend and his eldest brother.

After one roll had been taken, the tactful photographer chewed his gum as he replaced the film efficiently and said, "So." Snap. Crackle. "Let me get this straight. We're taking a couple of pictures without someone, eh?"

It seemed nobody knew what he was talking about, except one.

"That's right." The hushed voice seemed to be coming from *her* lips.

"Well, who is it? 'Cause I need to keep this session going." Apparently this small-town snapper was a busy man.

On a Sunday.

Oh dear, I thought, as I looked down at a broken fingernail. *I better take care of this before it snags . . .*

"Jen . . . " My name seemed to reverberate through the silence.

"Huh?" I snorted, with my fingernail between my teeth.

"Would you mind sitting these next few pictures out? We just want some of the *family.*"

I stopped my chewing as I watched each family head turn to face me, eyes pleading for me to do I'm-not-sure-what. Smile? Not make a scene? Cry and pee my pants? Everyone looked at me, with one exception: my boyfriend. I looked over to him, and *he* was looking down at *his* fingernails, fidgeting.

Despite six intimate years, four different apartments, one trip to Mexico and a massive joint CD collection, I left my seat slowly and humbly, trying to grab the emotional lifeline I knew deep down he was throwing out to me. I couldn't find it though. But it *was* there, just invisible, yeah, invisible that day. I made my way to the kitchen table, and for one full roll I played with the frilly edge of a pink place mat.

I licked my wounds in the following months. But it was no use. I heard it loud and clear.

"It's not you. It's me."

How dare he? I thought. *How dare he break up with me after all she put me through? Oh, terrific! He tells me this now? After a total of eight and a half years together? What about* my *dreams,* my *plans with* my *life? At least his mother had the decency to be honest about* her *feelings from the start. At least she never led me on.*

I felt as used as a soiled diaper. I felt as ignored as the dirty snow on my car tires. I had borne the brunt of her malice and his insensitivity and I was exhausted. My muscles felt strained from that heavy load; my skin stung like it had been raked over hot coals.

I didn't let him leave with much. I ended up keeping three quarters of our stuff, including the brand new sofa, the dishes and one of his mother's Chinese carpets.

The greatest irony of all is that she ended up choosing a family portrait with me in it. "The other ones looked like they had something missing," she said.

It's comforting to know that somewhere out there is an expensive portrait with *Jennifer* sitting right in the middle of everything, staining a perfect family moment. What a home-wrecker!

The Greek Geek and the Baklava

Ann Blondo

Often, romantic disasters sneak up on otherwise reasonable people when they let down their guard. Mine literally caught me with my pants around my knees. I was teetering, drunk, on the toilet of a newly opened yuppie microbrewery, trying to pull up my jeans, when my coworker Phil barged into the stall and kissed me. He was an engineer ten years my senior, who had noticeably perked up when I'd announced that Ben, my boyfriend of four years, and I had broken up the day before. I'd had a brief crush on Phil several years earlier, the way one has a crush on a high school teacher, the attraction based more on the pull of the exotic than on specific qualities. After my ex showed up at the bar, barely spoke to me and then disappeared in the throng of beer-guzzling frat boys, I was overcome with fear that I'd never be loved again. So, I did what any desperate girl would do. I waged a full-on charm assault on Phil, hoping a little flirtation would lift my spirits. Six mediocre pints of ale later, we were pressed against the rattling walls of the bathroom stall, my urine swirling down the toilet along with my good sense.

The next day at work he called me into his office to apologize. We laughed and let it go, promising a return to normalcy. Two days later we slept together. I had spent what felt like an eternity with Ben. I needed someone to redeem me fast, to show me that I wasn't going to die alone, that a boy who was responsible (irresponsibility being my primary grievance with Ben) could love me.

Soon we were spending almost every night together. For me, it was a strange compulsion, something I had to do to ward off the pain lingering at my shared-apartment doorstep. Ben was camping on the couch while he looked for a new living arrangement. Phil's bed kept me miles away from the carnage.

It also kept Phil and me far from the public eye. I didn't want to be seen with him. We were a secret at work because he was my superior, and a secret from my friends because I was ashamed. I knew my judgment had been faulty, both in timing and in taste. While I was embarrassed by my inability to be single, even for one night, I was even more embarrassed by Phil. I didn't appreciate his looks (before you brand me a superficial bitch, let me say I'm a firm believer that anyone is beautiful to someone who loves them). In my eyes, his hair was rodentlike. His teeth were gruesome; his loving smiles made me cringe. His jeans were much too tight. He thought that I, a midwestern head cheerleader, was very punk rock. He was amazed by my spontaneity, my love of loud music, my quirky style. It was as if I had sparked (or was a result of) a premature midlife crisis. He tried to be more like his distorted vision of me (young, hip, "alternative"), but he always got it wrong. His first courtship offering was a psuedo–Latin American glowing Virgin Mary gearshift knob for my car (very *not* my style), which he insisted on having installed immediately. Two days later my car reappeared with the offending item permanently welded to my gear stick, the base of the tacky orb wrapped in gobs of electrical tape. I was horrified, but since it was irreversible, I feigned gratitude.

I fought my discomfort with a pragmatic attitude: Maybe this was what grown-up love was like. After all, my father constantly embarrassed my mother with his lame jokes, his irrepressible farts, his awful outfits—and they'd been together thirty years. I attributed my squirms to emotional immaturity, worrying that if I let this one get away, I'd be forever stuck in the ghetto of reticent, inept indie-rock boys (like all the boys I thought were cute). Maybe Phil was a grown-up taste, like pâté. Maybe my heart just hadn't caught up to my head yet. Phil adored me. He acted as if he had won the lottery when we kissed. He told me all the things that Ben never did—that I was smart and beautiful and, after a few weeks, that he loved me. He did all of the right things, so why did I feel so *not* right?

In an effort to make him fit my script for the ideal adult relationship, I invited him to my family's annual vacation in the mountains of Colorado. In four years of dating, I had never invited Ben. But I thought I could make my new relationship succeed if I went through the proper motions. Maybe if we were away from my friends and the cute boys my age, I could see him as he really was—a loving, capable catch of a lifetime.

Having him among my family made me shudder even harder. He was auditioning for them, and this earnestness exacerbated his most cringe-worthy qualities. At the workplace I had noticed his loud, honking laugh, urgently pleading with the world to notice that he had a highly developed sense of humor. He always laughed longer and harder than anyone else, as if somehow he got the joke on a level impenetrable to the rest of us dullards. At least among the cubicles it was a relief from the drudgery. But up in the mountain air it was like a fire alarm, disturbing the peace in our rustic hideaway, breaking the flow of conversation. While his laugh was irritating, his own attempts at humor were downright insipid. First, he had a habit of recycling *my* jokes and expecting me to respond with hysterical laughter, as if I would find my own jokes funnier coming from someone else. He also liked to create his own captions for newspaper photos and rewrite lyrics to songs, Weird Al–style. He quickly rewrote my brother's favorite song, "Kicker of Elves," to be "Stocker of Shelves." He sang it over and over, while chopping vegetables or hiking in the forest, as if we hadn't heard him right the first twenty times, as if the already inane joke would age like fine wine. Phil was insistent with his "humor," leaving me with two options: to pretend I didn't hear his clever comment or to emit a false chuckle (like faking an orgasm) to end the misery. When I chose the latter, the half-hearted laugh, his face assumed a pose of comic rigor mortis: jaw open, overbite bared, eyes popping, like a gargoyle glowering at me to keep laughing. Harder! Longer!

However, in Colorado I also noticed more of his good qualities—he played Uno with my little brother for hours on end, he cooked amazing breakfasts, and he tolerated my father. In my moments of recoil, I felt like a juvenile asshole. This person was capable of partnership, support, good fathering. He could fix my car. He would take the kids to soccer and not complain. What was my problem? And then Phil would put a pair of boxers on his head and make faces, calling to anyone who would listen, "Hey! Hey! Take my picture! Heh-heh-heh!"

Our romance had begun in the fall, shortly after I returned from a solo trip to Europe (also the catalyst for my breakup with Ben). Phil's amazement at my courage to travel alone for two months inspired him to plan a trip of his own. If I could do it, so could he! Finalized, his itinerary consisted of two weeks in Italy and France with his mother, one day alone and two weeks with me in the Greek Islands. Not only did he pay for his mother's trip, but he paid for mine, grateful to be finally spending a fragment of his hefty salary. He purchased the tickets around Valentine's Day. Twenty-four hours later, I had my first freakout.

I wanted to go see my favorite band play. Although the idea of him accompanying me sent chills up my spine, the alternative seemed equally ridiculous. I had turned him on to the band—how could I tell him I thought the concert would be awkward with him in tow? Besides, we spent all of our time together. I had shut out most of my other friends. I was regularly lying about my weekend activities so as not to admit he existed. I ignored my dread and asked him to meet me at the show. I was sitting at a table with my (by then tenuous) friends when he walked in. He was sporting a too-small sweatshirt, his signature tight jeans and hiking boots. As he approached our table, he did a cheesy hand signal, some misguided hybrid between the heavy-metal salute and his own era's "hang loose," and said, *"Cómo estás,* dudes!" Then he tried to high-five me. I asked him to please sit down and then I introduced him to my friends. They all seemed confused as to his identity, but spared me the questions. He laughed too loud at our deadpan commentary, ordered a pitcher of "Burpmeister" (that's Budweiser to us unfunny folks) and generally made me wish a hurtling asteroid would take out the club.

Slowly, some of his friends arrived (each eliciting a high-five and "*cómo estás*" from Phil) and took a neighboring table. They all knew me well because he didn't hide me from his friends. I avoided eye contact with them, unwilling to integrate the two tables. His friends would surely mention outings we had all been on, and then my cover would be blown. Ironically, Phil's friends were far less embarrassing than he was. He had clearly appointed himself the token cool guy of the group, while they were content to be average working stiffs.

Finally, a couple of my pals asked if I wanted to go wander around. After assuring Phil I'd be back soon, I disappeared into the crowded band room . . . and never returned. When the show was over, I spotted him marching toward me through the sea of spilled beer, angrily kicking the stray cups in his path. He had been combing the club for half an hour. He was panicked and furious, and I had nothing to say for myself. Finally, I made a feeble gesture with my hands, as if to say, *Well, what do you expect?*

"I get it. You were embarrassed. You wanted to be cool in front of your friends, and that didn't include hanging out with me," he said.

I just sulked. He was right.

The next night I went out with my friends again. And then I cheated on Phil. Because that whole era entailed pretending things were different than they really were, denying the existence of my boyfriend for a night proved remarkably easy. When the offending Casanova and I got to the point in flirtation when a good girl says, "I have a boyfriend," I tested the line in my head. It sounded fundamentally inaccurate and so I never uttered it. I let nature take its course, as if I was an animal unencumbered by pesky morals. I told Phil the next day that things felt weird and that maybe we should break up (I didn't tell him about my infidelity). He left it up to me. When presented with the choice, I was scared. Did letting him go mean dismissing the possibility of a relationship with an adult? His lifestyle was so appealing: He had a house and a dog and a car and all of the things that no boys my age had. How could I kiss it goodbye? So I took a deep breath and squashed all of my uneasiness. I could train myself to love this person. I certainly loved the idea of him. Some of the time.

When he left for Italy, my relief was palpable. I received several lovely postcards, which instead of warming my heart made the hair on my arms stand on end. A week before I was to fly to Greece, I cheated on him again. The fact was, I just couldn't stand to turn down the attentions of another boy—a cute, interesting boy—to save myself for my dorky engineer.

I called my mother crying.

"Clearly, I don't want to be with him. I keep making out with other people."

"Do you want to go on the trip?"

"Not really, but what if I change my mind later? What if I'm making a terrible mistake? I have no way to reach him. Not showing up at the airport is pretty drastic."

"Look at the trip as a data-gathering mission. You'll only learn more after two weeks together. Then, whatever you decide, you'll be sure."

Could I really go on the quintessential romantic vacation

with a boy who made my skin crawl? It seemed so perverse. But I did want to see the hills of whitewashed houses, the sparkling sand, the fiery sunsets. I could pull it off. If anything could show me the error of my ways, it was Greece.

In the airport, the dread hit like a sudden wave of nausea. A moment later I heard a familiar voice bellow, *"Ciao bella!"* in a cheesy faux-Italian accent. Then his newly tanned arms were around me.

I knew I had made a big mistake.

The next two weeks dragged and dragged, romantic vista after romantic vista twisting a knife in my chest. It was so perfect—and so unbelievably wrong. He had gained a breezy confidence in his time away, and it compounded my revulsion. I couldn't stand this world traveler–guy persona—who the fuck did he think he was, Lawrence of Arabia? The smug look on his face as I sunned topless on the beach was like that of a paunchy insurance salesman beholding his new red Porsche.

One morning at the scooter-rental shop, we had an argument with the proprietor over whether or not our scooter was defective. I had, soon after arriving in Greece, developed the habit of uttering adolescent comments to no one in particular as a way to channel my inner disgust. I could be snotty to the trees, the sand, the clouds above, and it would save me from snapping at Phil. As we drove away from the irate scooter man, I said, in a valley girl accent, my fingers held in a *w,* "Whatever, Greek Dude."

Phil thought that was the funniest thing he'd ever heard. For the next few days, he would say the line over and over, or beg me to say it, and then he'd double over laughing, his face expectant. My forced chuckles made my heart wither.

But it was food that destroyed my hopes of reconciliation once and for all. First it was the Greek yogurt. Every morning he'd buy a container. And then he'd stir it for three minutes. It only took a couple of swirls to properly mix the honey and nuts in the yogurt, but something about the process was so compelling to him, he just couldn't stop. The sound of the spoon on the sides of the container was pure torture to me. But a piece of baklava was what finally made me break.

I am somewhat of a compulsive eater, I admit. Particularly when I am removed from a normal schedule, food takes on monumental importance. On vacation I obsess over when and what I will consume next. Add anxiety and discomfort to the mix, and one can see why I was eating like a lumberjack the entire trip. One afternoon I went for a walk, for a much-needed break from Phil, and bought an enormous piece of baklava. I ate half of it and saved the other half for Phil. Not because I wanted to, but because I thought I should. I was ashamed of my insatiable appetite; it reminded me of all of my other unchecked flaws, such as kissing random boys mere days before I went on vacation with my secret boyfriend. I brought the baklava back to our hotel, already regretting the decision to save it, and presented it to him. He set it on the bedside table and asked if I wanted to go to the beach. The pastry sat uneaten for the whole day. Every time I saw it, his refusal of my exceptional generosity incensed me. It was all I could think about. That night I dreamed he ate it, then I awoke startled, and it was still there, the moonlit night casting blue shadows in the crinkles of the waxed paper. I swore I could hear a faint ticking from inside the bag. The next morning, before I rolled out of bed, I stared at it again. I vowed that if Phil hadn't eaten it by dinnertime, I would shove it in my mouth right in front of him and slap his face if he so much as blinked.

That afternoon, while Phil was in the bath, I knew it was

time. I decided he didn't need to see me eat it—I could do it covertly. That way he would have to force the confrontation. He would look like the petty asshole and I could act wounded: *You're bothering me about eating some baklava? Geez, I didn't know it was so important.* I was reaching for the package when he called, "Hey honey, can you bring me the baklava?"

I was incredulous. Had I heard him right? What kind of fucking moron eats a pastry in the bathtub? Was this some sick joke?! I decided it was a sign from God. He was put on Earth to annoy the shit out of me.

I stepped into the bathroom, the package sticky in my palm. Phil turned off the water. He was curled naked in the tub.

"Look, I'm a fetus," he said.

"Yeah," I said, smiling weakly.

He was cracking himself up—again—and giving me that look. *A fetus! So funny! How could I not be rolling in the aisles? Where does this kooky, kooky guy come up with these things?*

I put the baklava on the rim of the sink and began to leave. But he insisted that I go get his camera and take a picture of him as a fetus. I sighed and got the camera. When I framed his body in the lens, he brought his thumb to his mouth. Next his eyes twinkled, my cue to laugh. But it took all I had just to press the button. Then I collapsed on the bed and prayed for deliverance.

When he emerged from the bath, he put on the same unfortunate shirt he had been wearing the entire trip. Only this time he decided to button only two buttons.

"Ready?" he asked, donning his idiotic Terminator sunglasses.

I glared up at him, my teeth clenched. "Whatever . . . Magnum P.I."

Did I just say that? Surely, I didn't.

He looked as if I had slapped his face, then said, "You know, it seems like you don't like me anymore."

I waited for a moment and said, "No . . . I do." I couldn't tell the truth. We had another week in paradise. Maybe I could still come around. I took a deep breath and closed my eyes. "I still like you. I'm just crabby. Sorry."

Of course, I didn't come around. I could have left early, or broken up with him in the airport at home, or at my front door, or on the phone when he returned to his house. But then there were his friends, who couldn't wait to hear about the trip. And my brother was coming to visit and asking for Uno rematches. And if I dumped him immediately, everyone would say, "You just used him for the free vacation." And would they be right? I don't know. In some ways I felt I let him use me. He had arbitrarily decided I was the one to fulfill his romantic fantasies. What better way to culminate that fantasy (or crush it) than with a standard-issue romantic trip? Maybe I was just playing along.

I cut him loose soon after the mandatory debriefings and visitors passed. (The thirty times he whipped out the fetus picture or forced me to say, "What-ever Greek Dude," aided my resolve.) I told him I needed time alone, that I should have taken time off before starting a new relationship. Post-split, work became hellish. After several weeks of awful encounters—him crying in the elevator, calling me into his office for coffee-break summits, browbeating me at the bus stop to quit my job—he held a secret meeting with our bosses. He sobbed and gave his resignation, citing me as the sole reason for abandoning the firm that had facilitated his career. Despite his testimony, my own job stayed intact, although I was branded a cruel Lolita. The management admitted Phil was not without blame; they clucked their tongues at his unmanliness and naiveté. He should have known better, they said.

I now understand what brought Phil and me together. We were each other's mirage, a projection of all the unfulfilled wishes we both had for love. He had been waiting for ten years for The One, whom he could take to Europe, laugh with and adore. I had been dreaming of a person who could give back, who appreciated my unique qualities and, mostly, someone who could take care of me for once. This collision of fantasies completely obscured the personal specifics, the lack of chemistry. It was like a mistake in assembling a jigsaw puzzle: Some pieces appear to be complementary shapes, but when you jam them together, the picture they make is clearly off.

With five years' distance, I cringe equally at his idiosyncrasies and my denial. I have blocked out the horrific aftermath of our breakup with the convenient mantra, *I did him a favor by letting him go.* And I mean it when I say, "That boy is going to make some lucky girl very happy." I just hope she likes to laugh. At anything. On cue.

Franklin's Fetish

Rebecca Morgan Frank

I t was the perfect meeting. I was standing in the upper entrance at the food co-op, passing out flyers for the upcoming Earth Day celebration. I had volunteered, not just for the discount, but for the opportunity to get involved in my new home. I had picked Albuquerque rather randomly off the map in a desperate attempt to escape the woman responsible for breaking my heart.

From my perch on the stairs I could watch all the shoppers, moving through the aisles, tossing items in their baskets and stopping to talk with friends. I had been standing there with my big stack of flyers for almost two hours when I saw her: the first woman to catch my eye since my tortuous breakup the year prior. She walked through the bulk section right over to the frozen foods and reached into the soy shelf. She was small, with ultrashort bleached hair and glasses; she was hip and sharp, and she even ate tempeh. I was enthralled.

I watched her shop, noting her thick black boots, her loosely belted jeans, her adorable swagger. My attraction increased as I witnessed her collecting a nice assortment of organic produce, bulk grains and herbal teas. As she headed toward the checkout lanes, I saw her pull a bright red Gerbera daisy from the big buckets at the front of the store and I sighed. She was taking a flower home to some lucky woman, and all I wanted was to be the one she was going home to.

I was so lost in my daydream that I hardly noticed her coming up the stairs with her arms full of bags and the daisy between her teeth. Oh that mouth! I gulped and smiled and tried to hand her a flyer, which of course she had no free hands to grab, so I stuck one in the top of her groceries. She nodded her thanks and disappeared.

I had barely let out my next sigh and was just beginning to engage in a good round of single-lesbian self-pity, when she came back in, holding only the Gerbera daisy. She handed it to me quickly, saying she had no one else to give it to, and ran out the door. By the time I had come to my senses, she was long gone, and only the soft red petals were there in my hand, telling me it was time to move forward with my new life.

I could tell you how I found Julie later at the bookstore where she worked, how we stayed up for hours at the bar that night, celebrating the fact that we were both vegan and feminists, and we both loved Alice Walker and Sarah McLachlan. I could tell you about that first whirlwind weekend she spent at my place. Because those were the moments I would like to remember. That was before I met the man in her life, Franklin.

Franklin was less than a foot tall, with a thick wrinkled face and a tendency to drool and snort constantly. Franklin was a little tan pug who garnered coos and pets from every passerby.

Julie was an ardent animal rights activist and an animal lover. I could relate. I fell for her small black kitten and her huge fluffy cat, who constantly tried to sleep on my head each night. I was wild about this woman and determined to fall in love with her whole animal kingdom. I was sure there must be some way I could learn to love Franklin.

Julie had introduced him to me with great pride.

"Here's my boy." She beamed down at him, as if she were looking at something exquisitely beautiful.

I tried to smile as he raced around me in circles, barking.

"Isn't he precious?"

"Precious" did not quite describe the wrinkled snorting creature jumping up on me. His dark round eyes protruded from a thick mass of wrinkles, which made him look like he'd run into a wall full speed.

"Adorable," I gulped. I would have told her anything, even as Franklin stared at me with those bug eyes, his mouth hanging open as he breathed and snorted as if he had a bad cold. Besides, I was sure I would come around to liking him. It wouldn't be long before I knew better.

The truth is, Franklin was rude. He would step and jump right over me whenever he pleased. When he leapt into my lap from the back seat and dug his claws into me every time Julie braked in her big Volvo, I smiled bravely as she praised his agility. I knew that the red welts rising on my legs would disappear before long. And when I woke up in the morning to the view underneath his curled upturned tail as he parked his stocky body on my chest in a quest to get to Julie, I remembered that while there was nothing more ugly than a pug butt, there was a beautiful woman on the other side of it.

I even endured his frenetic pacing around the bedroom as he raced about on his short little legs, intent on sniffing everything over and over again, each new discovery punctuated by a snort. His all-night journeys often took him in circles over our bodies as we lay in bed, his tiny feet delivering the impact of his weighty muscular body; this was a ritual that Julie seemed to sleep right through.

I soon learned that "Good morning, precious," was not meant for me, but for the gasping little body that plowed over me every morning. Sometimes he paused by my head, giving me a close-up of his small face, which seemed to work overtime trying to process the bodily fluids that came out of his nose and mouth in his labored effort to breathe. I cringed away from his attempts at good-morning kisses, and then watched Julie shower him with attention, which he received eagerly and with no regard for my physical presence on the bed.

"There's my boy! Oh you are so precious!"

"Ouch! He's standing on my stomach . . . "

"Oh, Franklin! He just wants to be near you—he likes you. Don't you, Franklin?"

Neither Franklin nor I ever responded.

Julie's ceaseless adoration for Franklin meant that he went everywhere that we went. This resulted in a total of two date options, the first of which was walking him to the nearby park, well known for its gang activity. The other involved sitting out-side at the local café, even when the desert air turned cool, so that Franklin could squat underneath our feet, tied to my chair and ready to eagerly pull and jump at each person who came toward the café door. It seemed that every woman who passed by needed to stop and comment on his unbelievable cuteness, while Julie smiled proudly and I tried to unwrap his leash from my legs or hold my chair steady as he pulled toward the women, playing cupid to these regular flirtations.

In Julie's eyes, Franklin deserved to have all the rights and privileges that she did, which meant unrestricted access to my own apartment. Franklin often peed inside her house and even christened my own apartment. I would run with him through my roommate's half of the house, praying he wouldn't stop to leave his mark. Once we safely reached my own door, I watched helplessly as he raced around my bedroom, his flat face pressed against every corner of my carpet. When he stepped onto my floor-level futon, I called his name with all the sweetness I could muster, knowing he would never listen. I knew what he had in mind.

The ruined bedding and carpet didn't seem to faze Julie, whose scoldings would often turn into an exchange of kisses with that wrinkled and wet flat face. I couldn't blame him for wanting her affections, and so I remained silent, waiting for my turn. In the midst of their love fests, she never noticed my pouts and my sighs, or the inevitable impatient tapping of my foot. But I could see the gleam of victory in Franklin's eyes as I stood alone, watching her smother him with affection just minutes after he had destroyed my room.

All of this I could have lived with. And maybe I could have gotten past the pungent smells his drool left on the pillowcases, and the stiff tan hairs that covered the sheets. But Franklin had an obsession with my panties, which I found hard to accept.

He preferred them dirty and would sniff mine out when Julie and I made love. He would even jump up and grab them from wherever I tried to carefully place my clothes before bed. I would wake up to find him chewing them at the end of the bed, or I would discover that he had strewn them somewhere else in the house, for all to see, once he had had his way with them. And so I would be forced either to put the soggy items back on my body or shove them in my pockets and wear nothing.

I tried to entice Franklin with delicacies in hopes that he would leave my underwear alone, but he only had a taste for one thing. I would wake up to the sound of sucking and chewing, and it was never of the circle of rawhide, or the organic carob bones, or the expensive fleece toy shaped like a squirrel that Julie had begged me to buy him. I had to fight him for the crumpled wet ball of fabric that had once been one of my most intimate and expensive items of clothing, and I inevitably felt less than victorious by the time I had pried the undergarment from his drooling mouth.

Franklin's fetish for the female undergarment was something that Julie herself seemed to find perfectly normal. There was never a scolding, but instead just an everyday, "Here, you forgot these," as she handed me Franklin's latest find as I walked out the door, straining to hear her voice over his excited and high-pitched barking.

It's a funny phenomenon, the pet owner. When you fall in

love with one, you are making a commitment not only to her, but to her companion animals. Any daydreams of the evolution of my relationship with Julie would eventually drift to the nightmare of moving in together, in which I would come home to Franklin every night, wake up to Franklin every morning, and Franklin would have unlimited access to my undergarments.

I tried to picture a place with a yard. I tried not to picture him running away, or meeting a premature end. I was not a mean person, so all my fantasies of his departure from our lives involved sticking him in a home where he had bigger yards, or his own supply of silk panties, or any other happy ending in which I could be rid of him, guilt-free. I tried to imagine Franklin changing, and then I tried to imagine Julie changing him. I knew there was no hope. I was tired of pulling out crumpled underpants with my change when I stopped at the co-op for groceries. I wasn't much of a dog person to begin with.

I'd like to say I was strong enough to break it off myself, or that Franklin and I went to family counseling. The truth is, Julie left me to go back to a girlfriend who treated her like dirt, and whom she discovered cheating on her with another woman in her kitchen a few months later. But by the time she came crawling back to me, saying leaving me was the biggest mistake she had ever made, I had come to my senses. I knew I would never be able to commit to Franklin.

Besides, I'd fallen in love and committed to someone else. And I was happily living with her beautiful, elegant Scotty, who was only interested in my used tampons.

Please Don't Vomit

Audra Wolfmann

We had just passed the second Mammoth Orange.

Please-don't-vomit-please-don't-vomit-please-don't-vomit-please.

My mind repeated this mixture of mantra and jingle as my brother drove my car eastbound on 152. I told him that he would have to drive if he wanted to get home for Passover because I had had several too many Ghetto Tangs the night before at Café Rick, and the mixture of vodka, peach schnapps and 7 UP was acting out the moves from a Busby Berkeley film inside my liver. He liked cinematic descriptions and asked no further questions. Besides, he always wants to drive my car. He's an epileptic or something and isn't allowed to have a license. I wasn't about to try to explain that the hangover was mostly induced from shame, a far more potent bile churner for me.

Please-don't-vomit-please-don't-vomit-please-don't-vomit-please.

"Wouldn't it be cool to live in one of those oranges?" my brother asked. "I mean, the commute to the city would be a bitch, but I could totally envision myself in one of those oranges."

He probably could. Nobody's even noticed those obscene, hollow roadside spheres since the 1960s, and my brother wants to live in one. He was possibly thinking that there was still some secret unlimited source of Orange Smoothy in there, flowing discretely for the past forty years.

He studied the shrinking fruit in the rearview mirror. "What do you think the rent would be on one of those babies?"

Please-don't-vomit-please-don't-vomit-please-don't-vomit-please.

I wanted to tell him to watch the road but I was afraid to open my mouth. You see, the thing about vomit is that it's a stealthy hombre that takes advantage of any opportunity to come to town. Did I just say *"hombre?"*

Please-don't-vomit-please-don't-vomit-please-don't-vomit-please.

"I mean, it's got to be a lot less than my apartment—and my apartment isn't even shaped like an orange! Do you think girls like guys who live in empty produce? It might just be the gimmick I've been looking for. Oh, did I tell you about the prime hottie that came into the comic-book store the other day? She knew all about the early issues of *Doom Patrol,* and she had this pink hair and a set of *knaydl* like you wouldn't fucking believe."

If I allowed myself the supreme joy of vomiting, the ecstasy of ralphing, the forbidden fruit of Yak . . .

Please-don't—

"But Mom says girls don't go for guys once they're in their thirties unless they own property. I guess I should buy one of the Mammoth Oranges."

I squeezed my eyes shut as tightly as my face could squash them. If I could only concentrate on my brother's infernal drone, I might be able to abandon the mantra. The more I chanted, the more it became apparent to me that the mere repetition of the repetitious chant was enough to render the endeavor futile. Furthermore and more specifically, the word "vomit" has a rather adverse effect on the throat and stomach muscles I was attempting to repress.

Please-don't—

"You're lucky. You got all the good looks in the family. When am I going to meet a nice girl? Girls like gimmicks. I should get a Vespa. Like that guy you went out with last night. That's why you like him, right? Art student on a Vespa equals big old gimmick."

Why my brother was attempting social critique upon the canvas of my private life at a time like that, I'll never understand. Caleb and his Vespa were exactly what I was trying not to think about. The pressure in my intestines surged into my esophagus.

Please-don't—

"So he's an artist? An *artiste?* Probably thinks no one understands him. Probably likes Jeff Koons. That bastard."

As I squashed my eyes together, sparks and swirls of images appeared. I saw airplanes crashing and animated van Goghs and some sort of cerebral fireworks show all taking place under the proscenium of my eyelids. The slow, hollow burning in my stomach that I felt the night before as I left Caleb's apartment never quite went away. In fact, it had spread the entire length of my body, extending itself to the insides of my bones and the tips of my hair. He was probably drinking coffee at this moment with some Art Institute tramp, unaware of what I had done or where I was.

Please-don't—

It was hard to believe that I had met Caleb only a month earlier. My friend Dora dragged me to one of those chromatically themed bars for a post–art opening party. She didn't drag me to the art show, which was at some new space called Disturbo 2000, because, as she said, the post-party is where it all happens. I was single, unemployed and hadn't left the house in a week. How could I say no? Everything inside the bar was dark red except for the drinks, which were mostly light red and blue. The bar must have been the hottest attraction for the frontal-lobeless elite. As I looked around the womblike interior, I was met by half a dozen lobotomized stares that were something between flirtatious and derogatory. I couldn't tell. Dora was wrapped up in a conversation about "post-postmodernism" with a man in a floral-print dress when I decided to step outside for some multihued scenery.

"God knows where you find these guys."

I was aware of someone following me as I made my way through the bar, but I tried my best not to turn around and look. I was prepared to be disappointed or frightened by whomever was behind me, but I felt more inclined toward the possibility that this situation was a turning point in my destiny. This could be The One behind me. I've been told that it happens like that sometimes, especially when you're lonely and tell yourself that you are "not looking," as if that were ever possible. I threw open the plush red padded doors with as much eccentric drama as I could rationally muster in public and then demurely posed against the nearest lamppost, pantomiming a search for a pack of cigarettes that I didn't have because I've never smoked. I slowly looked up to see a woman thrusting my sweater in my face. "Here," she said. "You dropped this back in the bar."

I accepted my sweater and, as the woman turned to walk back into the bar, a man emerged behind her. He was very tall and slouchy, which I have always found attractive, and he had those traditional Semitic good looks that only the goyim have. He offered me a cigarette and I took it to add validity to the earlier pantomime. We looked at each other and smiled nervously for a while as I took overly anxious and frequent drags on his terribly cheap brand of cigarettes. He asked me if I'd seen his show that night at Disturbo 2000. I somehow had sensed that he was that night's featured artist. I didn't know any artists in real life, but sometimes I would walk by the Art Institute and stare in wonder, treating it like some kind of people zoo.

"Does Mom know you hang out with these weirdoes? I mean, come on! You and a biker?! Well . . . whatever you call a guy on a Vespa, besides 'gimmick' that is."

When I somewhat ashamedly said no, I hadn't seen his show, he walked me down the street and opened the closed gallery with his own key. There was a tense moment or two in the dark before he found all the light switches, when I wondered what the hell I was doing there, but then all at once the room was illuminated and mine eyes beheld . . . a grad student's art show. But the paintings were extremely well done—twenty canvases thick and chunky with expressionistic renditions of tractors. He confided to me that all the paintings were done from the same photo he clipped from an ad for a pumpkin patch. He grew up the son of an art dealer in New York City, and he had never seen a tractor before. Normally, I would have found myself laughing my skinny, inartistic ass off at how "typical" he was, but instead I stared deep into his red-rimmed blue eyes and told him how amazing he was.

I didn't have an art. Sure, I wrote articles and two-bit reviews of clothing stores for a neighborhood newspaper, but they were easy and I cranked them out mechanically. His paintings, by contrast, showed a deeply tortured spirit with visions of truth and beauty. I looked at him with a confusing mixture of admiration and lust, two emotions I often confused.

Caleb explained the theory behind his genius for hours and before I knew it, it was 6 A.M. and we were in his bed looking through an Otto Dix book. I'm not sure if I told him anything about myself, and I'm not sure if I understood a word he said, but it didn't matter. I was in love and he soon became my new hobby. I told everyone I knew about the ingenious new painter I had met, and waited tensely for his follow-up phone call that would prove that what we'd had wasn't a one-night stand.

"Why do women always go for these creeps? These self-proclaimed geniuses without a fucking clue. I've seen it happen a million times. Their girlfriends support them while they contemplate man's inhumanity to them."

When an entire week had passed, I decided that I hated Caleb and all the scourge of the Earth like him. It became brilliantly evident that we really didn't have anything in common, and I remembered that he in fact hadn't asked anything about me. He didn't know if I had siblings or cancer or anything like that. He couldn't possibly be The One. The One would have asked those questions. I was over him. However, on the eighth day, he called just before midnight and my hobby was rekindled. He explained how busy he was creating new works for his next show and how he had thought about me often. His voice was scratchy from too many cheap cigarettes and he sounded vaguely drunk. He said, "You can come over if you want." I rode my bike over to his rambling Victorian apartment despite the late hour, eager to pick up where we had left off the week before. And that's exactly where we ended up . . . in his bed, but this time with an Edward Hopper book.

As Caleb turned the pages of the oversized Hopper book and pointed out shadows and shading, I noticed how most of the paintings were devoid of humans, and the ones that had a woman or two in them were devoid of eye contact. It was as if the subjects of Hopper's paintings were ashamed to be in such a sterile environment and couldn't bring themselves to meet the viewer's gaze. I liked the paintings, but it was all somehow disconcerting. I asked Caleb if all of Hopper's paintings were so detached from humanity. He disagreed that it was indicative of a detachment from anything; he thought it was just style. He also vaguely remembered there being one portrait somewhere in Hopper's oeuvre with full frontal eye contact, but it wasn't in any of the books he had at his apartment. The images of empty Adirondack chairs and the sides of icy blonds' heads haunted me as we spent the weekend together.

"If I got a girl to go out with me, I'd take full responsibility and pay for all her meals. I'd never let a woman support me . . . well, excluding Mom."

During that weekend we went for walks, to the museum on a Caleb-guided tour and out to an impressive restaurant where he ordered and I paid. There were a few odd silences and nervous attempts on my part to keep the conversation going, but by Sunday morning I decided the weekend was turning out to be an important one despite the uncomfortable sense I had that I wasn't really me the whole time. I didn't want to ruin it by overstaying my welcome, so I suggested that I go home. My plants were probably dying anyway. He said that he liked having me around and that I should stay so we could go to a movie. We sat at his kitchen table for a few minutes. He seemed tense and then abruptly stood up. He said he had to run up to his studio "for just a minute." Since his studio was in his attic, I thought maybe he left something up there that he needed. Half an hour passed and his roommate Erica came in to make lunch. She was an acupuncturist for household pets and wore a crystal. We didn't have much to say to each other, but I guess she felt obliged to keep me company and refill my tea. After three hours I excused myself and found my way up the rickety ladder that led to Caleb's studio. He stood in front of a large brown canvas with a paintbrush in his mouth and one in his hand. He had forgotten all about me. I told him I was leaving in a tone that implied "for good." All he had to say was, "Bye."

At this point, I not only hated him but I also hated myself for having the low self-esteem to get myself in that situation. Here I was clamoring for attention from a tree stump. I heard the phantom voices of my parents' bygone advice: "Men think, why buy the cow when you can have the milk for free?" Why buy the cow indeed . . . or better yet, why even acknowledge the cow's humanity? It's not that I wanted to be bought, which I have always assumed means marriage. Marriage to me is sort of like skiing; I know lots of other people get all excited about it and plan their lives around it, but it has just never occurred to me as something I want to do. It just sounds too much like work. What "buying the cow" in this instance meant to me was realizing that someone's time is as valuable as yours, even if she is not an artist.

"You know, Mom and Dad are going to want to see some goddamned grandkids before they kick the bucket, and it's not looking too good for me, Bratso. You should really start looking at men as genetic investments."

I decided I was through with Caleb, yet I thought about him constantly. The rejection I felt was incomplete and inconclusive. He never told me to beat it, but rather expected me to have no feelings, like he did. I tried. When Caleb called a week later, I said I was busy. But when he showed up at my apartment anyway, I could not turn him away. Instead I allowed him to sit in a chair in my bedroom while I paced and gave him the silent treatment. Finally sensing that something was wrong, he illustrated with examples from history how artists are often self-absorbed. He told me how Jackson Pollock ruined the lives of all those around him, but how he still meant well. Caleb then began to tell me of Michelangelo's personal life but got sidetracked into describing the genius of his later paintings.

I interrupted Caleb to ask him if he had ever heard of the term *Menschlichkeit*. He hadn't and asked if it was a school of architecture. "No," I said. I explained that it's a very complicated Yiddish word, but basically it means being human and knowing what that means in relation to others. He looked confused and then, in an oddly proud and self-satisfied tone, said that he was a selfish person. I blinked at him for a few minutes, expecting there to be more, but there wasn't. "Well, this isn't AA, so admitting your problem isn't enough," I said and then asked him to leave.

My friend Dora called and asked how it was going with Caleb. I said, "He comes, he goes, he talks of Michelangelo." It's easy to be tough and literary about love trauma on the phone to a girlfriend.

Last night he showed up at my door again.

Please-don't—

"Yeah, if you get married and have a load of kids, Mom will totally get off my back!"

My brother likes the romantic notion that Mom and Dad are anxiously awaiting his wedding day, but in all honesty, our parents stopped holding their breath the moment he entered his thirtieth year of preadolescence. They reluctantly accepted his life of collector's edition comic books, thirteen-sided dice and all-night role-playing sessions with the guys, just as the parents of my gay friends accepted their children's lifestyles, with a resignation of their hope for grandchildren. Our parents' hope is still alive for me, but that burden is enough to be sterilizing.

"So, are you going to see this guy again or what?"

I wasn't. I really wasn't. I had promised myself that being alone wasn't as bad as being in the company of someone who didn't appreciate me. I decided that I needed to date myself for a while. That would be the only way to get back in touch with what it was that made me compulsively want to hang out with this guy who was so obviously wrong for me. Being lonely isn't an excuse for wasting time and self-esteem. But then, there he was last night, and somehow he seemed like a better alternative to an action-packed date with myself, my brother and maybe Sartre's *Being and Nothingness*. I got on the back of Caleb's Vespa as my brother walked up with a pizza.

"I thought we were going to hang out last night."

Instead, I waved goodbye to my perplexed brother, and we road to Caleb's favorite bar, Café Rick, which was a smelly dive that allowed smoking despite California law. It seemed that as a result of the lawlessness, people went insane and smoked two to three cigarettes at a time. Café Rick was running a two-for-one special on Ghetto Tangs last night, and apparently Caleb loves a deal. As an hour passed and the empty glasses piled up and the ashtray overflowed, we both got rapidly sloshed. Random women with geometric haircuts approached Caleb and effusively reminisced about old times, then moved on. I really had no idea who this guy was.

I had heard the expression "narrowing your eyes," but I don't think I had ever done it until last night. Through the narrowing of one's eyes, truth becomes apparent. Through drunk and narrow eyes, truth makes one belligerent. I really hated this guy and I was going to make him pay. I reached for my fifth Ghetto Tang and slurred, "Why'd you come over? What made you think that I'd want to see you again after last time?" He reached for his sixth Ghetto Tang and raised his eyebrows in a question mark as he drank. "I dunno," he said. "I guess you're just good that way."

It dawned on me all at once that I was. I was just another one of those girls who would come up to him in a bar one day and remember when. I just had never imagined that I could be someone's . . . casual good time. The room seemed to dim, and silence rang in my ears as I recognized the sensation that was running through my bones as embarrassment. How could I have thought that he would be capable of anything more than a halfhearted fling? "Bastard," I whispered unconsciously. I stood up and staggered toward the door, tripping over people in the dense smoke of the seedy bar. He followed after me and asked innocently, "Where are you going?" I told him that I was going home and he should really never come over to my place or call again. He seemed confused for a minute, then shrugged and offered me a ride home. Since I didn't have any money left for a cab, I accepted his helmet and we got on his Vespa.

It started to rain as we sped through the dark streets, and visions of being killed in a drunken Vespa accident became vivid to me. I clenched my eyes shut in a panic for minutes, hours, I'm not sure. When we stopped, I opened my eyes and saw that we were at his place and not mine. He explained that he was too drunk to drive all the way to my house and that I could just sleep over at his place. "No way," I said. "I'll walk." But the rain was getting harder and my physical discomfort won out over my mental discomfort.

"Hey Bratso, are you listening to me?"

As soon as we were in Caleb's room, he collapsed on his bed. I went over and yelled in his ear, but he was out cold. I paced in a rage of hatred. I'm not supposed to get into these kinds of predicaments! I'm respectable. Men chase me and throw flowers at my feet! (Well, it's never actually happened that way, but in theory it should have.) Here I was, wet and stranded in a place I never should have been in the first place. I hated him and I decided I needed revenge.

As I woozily scanned his room, my eyes fell on his bookshelf first. I could always rip pages out of those expensive art books he gloated over or maybe put a piece of luncheon meat between each page. I grabbed the Hopper book first, but then dropped it when I saw his slides on his desk. He was planning to send them to one of those grant contests. What if I drew stick figures on them with that Magic Marker that was lying conveniently close by? No, no. Too obvious. What if I just cut off some of his floppy artist hair and shoved it down his pants? Yeah! That would really freak him out in the morning. I rifled through his desk, looking for a pair of scissors. I wasn't having any luck finding them and was getting more and more frustrated. I started to cry and allowed myself to slide to the floor. I couldn't believe what was happening to me. I didn't hate him. I hated myself.

I closed the front door to Caleb's apartment quietly. The rain was sharp and freezing as it pelted my face. I had really seen a side of myself that I was not proud of that night. Walking in the stinging rain was a much-needed penance for me. I deserved this torture so I would remember the depths to which I could . . . I stopped in the middle of the street. Something hilarious had occurred to me. I spun around and ran all the way back to Caleb's apartment. The door was still unlocked so I let myself in and crept up the stairs to his attic studio. The painting he had been working on most recently was a nude, a young girl reclining on a tractor. I grabbed a tube of black paint and formed a mustache on her seductive face, mimicking Marcel Duchamp's all-too-familiar diss of da Vinci's *La Gioconda*. He always said Duchamp was overrated!

If a car is driving east going sixty-five miles per hour and a surge of sickness is slowly creeping northward through the esophagus of a twenty-four-year-old female, will the forward horizontal position actually slow the progress of the creeping, crawling illness?

"What are you doing? Are you gonna puke? Just fooling around, Bratso? Well, as I was saying . . . "

Please-don't—

"I don't think you should see that guy anymore. I hate that guy."

Please-don't—

"I mean, I really hate that guy."

Contributors

Isadora Alman, the "Ask Isadora" of the syndicated sex and relationship column that appears in the *San Francisco Bay Guardian, Philadelphia City Paper* and elsewhere, is a board-certified sexologist and a California-licensed marriage and family therapist. You can participate in her free, interactive website, Sexuality Forum, at www.askisadora.com.

Ann Blondo has an MFA and a terrific publication track record, but we won't go into specifics.

Judy Campbell is a public radio producer and reporter in San Francisco.

Holly Wisniewski Case is a freelance writer living in Fort Worth, Texas. She finally figured out that punk ideals are not about a dress code, and settled down with a guy who never sniffs his jacket. She's raising two young boys whom she hopes will not grow up to be punk rock sex gods.

When she's not airing her rooms, **Lauren Dockett** is a freelance journalist who writes short stories and nonfiction books for women. A contributing writer to *Girlfriends* magazine, she is the author of *The Deepest Blue: How Women Face and Overcome Depression*, and the coauthor of *Facing 30: Women Talk About Constructing a Real Life and Other Scary Rites of Passage* and the coming forth *Sex Talk*.

Allison Fraiberg is an associate professor of Liberal Studies at the University of Redlands in Southern California, where she teaches courses in American literature, critical thinking, and environmental studies. Her published work has appeared in such journals as *Postmodern Culture, Works and Days, Pedagogy, College Literature* and *Feminist Collections*. Her most recent work has focused on American women's performance comedy.

Rebecca Morgan Frank lives in the Boston area, where she is pursuing an MFA in creative writing at Emerson College.

Her poems have been published or are forthcoming in *Red River Review* and *Many Mountains Moving*. She recently gave in to her partner's pleading for a new puppy.

R. Gay is a writer and whatnot whose work can be found past, present and future in *Does Your Mama Know?*, *Love Shook My Heart 2*, *Herotica 7*, *Moxie magazine*, *Clean Sheets*, *Scarlet Letters*, *Best Bisexual Women's Erotica*, *The Sweet Life* and other publications.

Michelle Goodman is a freelance writer and editor living in Seattle. Her writing has appeared in print in alternative weeklies and in-flight magazines. Her writing has appeared online in *Salon*, *Playboy*, *Guru* and a handful of websites that have tanked. Michelle hasn't had what her family would call a real job in ten years and wishes more of her friends would join her in the pursuit of all things non-9-to-5. To help further her cause, she's written the handbook *In the Driver's Seat: A Roadmap for Freelancers*.

Jennifer Hacock plays piano and writes stories. Her current boyfriend's mother likes her.

A. C. Hall contributed to the Seal Press anthologies *Yentl's Revenge: The Next Wave of Jewish Feminism* and *The Unsavvy Traveler: Women's Comic Tales of Catastrophe*. For both, she wrote about her best sweetheart. She is very pleased not to write about him for a book about break-ups. Formerly a contributing writer for Seattle's wackiest alternative paper, *The Stranger,* her writing has also appeared in *The Seattle Times* and *Seattle Weekly*.

A boozy housewife living in Maine, everything **Antonia B. Johnston** writes is part of a coded, intricate web of lies. When not doing standup comedy and surrogate womb-work, she lifts weights and works on her novel that is already being optioned for a Hollywood film.

Rekha Kuver is currently working for a nonprofit organization. Her never-ending migratory experiences include moving from her birthplace, Flint, Michigan, to locations all over the Midwest, visiting and revisiting her parents' first home in Fiji, and working as a dancer, editor, mallworker, sound board operator, actor, stage manager, canoe renter and more. She currently lives in Seattle, searching for a Midwest-style, well-made doughnut.

Megan Lambert lives in Northampton, Massachusetts, with her partner, four-year-old son, a temperamental cat, and, as of the writing of this piece, her very pregnant younger sister. Her first essay was published in *Breeder: Real-Life Stories from the New Generation of Mothers*, and forthcoming works will appear in *Bookbird, Proud Parenting* and a literary journal published by Simmons College.

Alison Luterman's first book, *The Largest Possible Life*, won the Cleveland State University Poetry Center Prize 2000. She lives in Oakland, teaches as a poet in the schools and is writing a play about sisters.

Elizabeth Mathews is a bookseller and freelance editor. She has been published by Poetry.com. She recently graduated from the Evergreen State College and now lives in Seattle, where she is working on becoming a cat lady.

M. Jane McKittrick eventually met Mr. Right on the corner of Bleecker and MacDougal. They live with their two children in the Pacific Northwest.

Lori Oliva is a writer and an independent public relations consultant living in Atlanta, Georgia. She frequently writes about business issues, and this is her first essay that focuses on the perils of a doomed personal relationship.

Gina Ranalli is an ex-New Englander, an ex-smoker and a recovering compulsive liar. Her power animal is the elusive Walnut-Turtle.

Vy Rhodes is the pen name of a full-time writer and editor who has finally found true love. To her delight, although he doesn't belch very often, he does squash spiders and perform oil changes.

Longtime Seattle resident **Elizabeth Schilling** now spends her evenings writing about her travel adventures rather than conducting affairs of the heart. During the day, she does public relations for a local electric utility company.

Audra Wolfmann currently lives in San Francisco and has an MFA in Creative Writing from Mills College. Although often technically unemployed, Audra writes short fiction, models, and has appeared in a few indie films you may, or may never, see. She is currently in the process of trying to interest publishers in her collection of short stories, "Fresno Noir." Her hobbies include maintaining a vast collection of vintage erotica on her website (www.audrawolfmann.com), eating burritos, and trying to find out what that weird smell is in her apartment. She has also taken up a sudden interest in metaphysics upon finding out that her aura is actually a chalk outline.

Zonna is 41 and living in New Yawk—Can you tell from her accent? Her short stories have appeared in anthologies by Alyson Publications (*Skin Deep; Dykes with Baggage; My Lover, My Friend),* Arsenal Pulp Press *(Hot & Bothered 2* and *3)* and Black Books *(Tough Girls).* When she isn't writing, she's usually changing her cat's litter box.

About the Editor

Kristin Beck, a freelance writer and editor, is the coauthor of *Facing 30: Women Talk About Constructing a Real Life and Other Scary Rites of Passage* (New Harbinger, 1998) and *The Self-Nourishment Companion: 52 Inspiring Ways to Take Control of Yourself* (New Harbinger, 2001). Her essays have appeared in *The Unsavvy Traveler: Women's Comic Tales of Catastrophe* (Seal Press, 2001) as well as various women's publications. She lives with her husband and their two young kids in Seattle.